To Dad
from
Dale

Xmas '80

NORTHERN

ITALIAN

COOKING

NORTHERN ITALIAN COOKING

by Francesco Ghedini

Decorative Drawings by Ed Nuckolls

GRAMERCY PUBLISHING COMPANY
New York

This edition is published by Gramercy Publishing Company,
a division of Crown Publishers, Inc.,
by arrangement with Hawthorn Books, Inc.
a b c d e f g h
GRAMERCY 1979 EDITION
Manufactured in the United States of America

Library of Congress Cataloging in Publication Data

Ghedini, Francesco.
Nothern Italian cooking.
Includes index.
1. Cookery, Italian. I. Title.
TX723.G43 1979   641.5'945   79-16065
ISBN 0-517-29599-7

CONTENTS

EDITOR'S NOTE

I have been waiting for this collection of recipes to be published for the past five years. It is an incomplete collection—Francesco Ghedini died within weeks after receiving a contract, but the recipes that he finished writing are truly exceptional and memorable. When I first became aware of this manuscript, I promptly copied my favorite recipes to test at home. My motives then for trying to get this book published were purely selfish ones; my copied recipes have since become food-stained and tattered.

However, it is about time that a Northern Italian cookbook was published in this country for the ever-growing number of traveling Americans who have had trouble leaving behind the fine food found in the restaurants of Florence, Genoa, Bologna, Milan, and Venice and have only their memories of the food specialties found on the tables in the countryside villages of Lombardy, Tuscany, Liguria, and Marche-Umbria.

These Northern Italian regions have helped to create a cuisine that is comparable to those of France and China. The dishes are tremendously colorful, and, as Ghedini once said, they are "effective in appearance as well as taste." In fact, there is almost an Oriental blending of colors, flavors, textures, and tastes. Characteristic ingredients include the combined use of olive oil and sweet butter; fresh herbs, such as parsley, basil and garlic; sauces made of tomatoes, stock, cream, wines, and wine vinegars; delicate cheeses such as fontina and Fiore Sardo, Romano and Parmesan; *zampone, cotechino,* and mortadella sausages; prosciutto; and special touches of walnuts and lemon peel.

I know very little about the author, Francesco Ghedini, whom I met for a brief moment only once—before I ever read his cookbook and tried his recipes. I have learned that he was an Italian nobleman who came to this country as a journalist specializing in food. He represented several Italian newspapers. While he was reporting from New York, he wrote food articles for American magazines and worked as a food consultant for the Italian cookbooks published in the Time–Life series. He also helped Luigi Carnacina, the last of the great European chefs, with two of the cookbooks that were published in this country. Mr. Ghedini married an American woman with whom he was very much in love but who died of cancer shortly after their marriage. Ghedini was so overcome with grief that he committed suicide soon after her death. The only thing that Ghedini left behind was *Northern Italian Cooking.*

It has been a special pleasure to edit this manuscript, test the recipes, and watch this book finally come to fruition. I have not, in many cases, written strict translations of the Italian titles for the recipes; I thought it would be more helpful for the American cook to know the content of the dishes. Often Ghedini discusses the titles—especially when they are part of a local dialect—and origins of the dishes in his introductions to the recipes. I hope cookbook readers and cooks enjoy this book as much as I have.

Elizabeth Backman

SAUCES

SALSE

Quattro Spezie

Salsa Besciamella

Polpa al Pomodoro
Salsa al Pomodoro
Salsa al Pomodoro alla Semplice
Salsa al Pomodoro a Crudo
Purea al Pomodoro

Sugo di Carne
Salsa al Marsala

Salsa alla Bolognese

Salsa Maionese
Salsa Citronette
Salsa Verde
Pesto alla Genovese
Salsa Vinaigrette

Salsa al Cioccolato

QUATTRO SPEZIE
FOUR SPICES

This mixture of four spices should be prepared and put in a jar on your spice shelf. Used in moderation, it is an excellent addition to various sauces and other dishes.

8 tablespoons freshly ground white pepper
2 tablespoons freshly grated or ground nutmeg
2 tablespoons freshly ground juniper berries
2 teaspoons ground cloves

Mix well together and use when indicated.

MAKES ABOUT ¾ CUP

SALSA BESCIAMELLA
BÉCHAMEL SAUCE

2 tablespoons sweet butter
3 tablespoons flour
2 cups hot milk
½ teaspoon salt
¼ teaspoon freshly ground white pepper
¼ teaspoon freshly grated or ground nutmeg
Bouquet garni: 1 crushed bay leaf and ½ teaspoon thyme

1. Melt the butter in a saucepan over low heat and blend the flour into it.
2. Slowly stir in the hot milk. Then season with salt, white pepper, and nutmeg.
3. Add the bouquet garni. Cook and stir constantly with wire whisk, until smooth and boiling. Cook 2 minutes longer and remove bouquet garni.

MAKES ABOUT 2 CUPS

POLPA AL POMODORO　　　　　*North Italy*
TOMATO PULP

3 *pounds firm, ripe tomatoes*

1. Dip tomatoes in boiling water for 10 to 12 seconds. Remove, peel, and cut in half.
2. Squeeze each half gently to get rid of seeds and water, then, if necessary, use the handle of a spoon to dig out remaining seeds.
3. Chop fine and let stand, in bowl, for about 20 minutes. Drain thoroughly and use as directed.

MAKES ABOUT 4½ CUPS

NOTE: If tomatoes are not in season and fully ripe, canned imported Italian plum tomatoes, which are already peeled, may be substituted, but must be thoroughly drained, with seeds removed, chopped, and then drained again.

SALSA AL POMODORO　　　　*Emilia-Romagna*
TOMATO SAUCE

This Tomato Sauce may be served hot with any pasta, polenta, or gnocchi, and as an ingredient in other dishes as directed in recipes.

4 *pounds firm, ripe tomatoes*
1 *teaspoon salt*
1½ *tablespoons olive oil*
3½ *ounces lean prosciutto, chopped or ground*
1 *medium yellow onion, finely chopped*
¼ *teaspoon dried thyme*
1 *bay leaf, crushed*
1 *tablespoon flour*
¼ *teaspoon freshly ground black pepper*
½ *teaspoon sugar (more, if tomatoes are bitter)*
1 *tablespoon sweet butter (optional)*

1. Dip tomatoes in boiling water for 10 to 12 seconds. Remove, peel, and cut in half. Squeeze each half gently to get rid of seeds and water; then, if necessary, use the handle of a spoon to dig out remaining seeds. Sprinkle the interiors with the salt, which will draw out even more water; invert them in a colander and let stand and drain for about 20 minutes. Chop and set aside.

2. Heat olive oil in a 2-quart saucepan. Add prosciutto, onion, thyme, and bay leaf. Sauté, over low heat, until onion is golden.

3. Remove saucepan from heat, sprinkle mixture with flour and stir until well mixed. Place back on very low heat and simmer for a few seconds, stirring constantly.

4. Add thoroughly drained, chopped tomato pulp. Season with pepper and sugar and stir well. Bring to a simmer and cook, over low heat, for 30 minutes, or until thickened, stirring frequently, especially as sauce thickens. Remove from heat. If you like a richer and creamy taste stir in 1 tablespoon butter. Purée mixture in blender or food mill.

MAKES ABOUT 2½ CUPS

SALSA AL POMODORO ALLA SEMPLICE   *North Italy*
EASY TOMATO SAUCE

This sauce, which is so simple and easy to prepare, is very fresh and light. It is devoid of all oregano and garlic to which most Americans are accustomed in Southern Italian sauces. In many cases, as will be indicated, this sauce should be diluted either with chicken broth or water.

6 tablespoons sweet butter
1 medium yellow onion, coarsely chopped
½ cup coarsely chopped celery
½ cup coarsely chopped carrots
4 heaping cups Polpa al Pomodoro *(Tomato Pulp)*, page 4, or
    4 cups canned imported Italian plum tomatoes, drained, with
    seeds removed, and chopped
1 teaspoon salt
¼ teaspoon freshly ground black pepper
2 tablespoons finely chopped fresh parsley
2 tablespoons finely chopped fresh basil *(if in season)* or 1 tea-
    spoon dried basil

1. Melt 4 tablespoons of the butter in a 2-quart saucepan. Add the onion, celery, and carrots and sauté, stirring, over low heat, until the onion is almost golden. Add the Tomato Pulp or the canned tomatoes, salt, and black pepper. Bring to a boil, lower heat, and simmer, stirring occasionally, for 20 minutes.

2. Add the parsley, basil, and the remaining 2 tablespoons butter. Stir and cook briefly until the butter has dissolved.

MAKES 3½ CUPS

SALSA AL POMODORO A CRUDO   *North Italy*
COLD TOMATO SAUCE

Cold Tomato Sauce is excellent served with cold meats and poultry, fish, shellfish, and with the only recipe of cold pasta in this book, *Tagliolini Freddi* (Cold Thin Egg Noodles), page 67.

3 cups finely chopped Polpa al Pomodoro *(Tomato Pulp) page
4, or 3 cups canned imported Italian plum tomatoes, drained,
with seeds removed, and finely chopped*
1 clove garlic, peeled
¼ teaspoon ground sage
1 teaspoon salt
¼ teaspoon freshly ground black pepper
2 tablespoons sweet butter, softened
Salt and freshly ground black pepper to taste

1. Place Tomato Pulp or canned tomatoes, garlic, sage, salt, and black pepper in a double boiler and cook, without boiling and stirring, until all ingredients are well mixed together.

2. Add butter, bit by bit, and stir until well mixed. Remove from heat, discard garlic, and chill.

3. Taste for seasoning, and purée in blender briefly.

MAKES ABOUT 3½ CUPS

PUREA AL POMODORO   *North Italy*
TOMATO PUREE

4 pounds firm, ripe tomatoes
2 teaspoons salt
3 tablespoons finely chopped yellow onion
1 large bay leaf

1. Dip tomatoes in boiling water for 10 to 12 seconds. Remove, peel, and cut in half. Squeeze each half gently to get rid of seeds and water, then, if necessary, use the handle of a spoon to dig out remaining seeds. Sprinkle the interiors with the salt, which will draw out even more water; invert them in a colander and let stand and drain for about 20 minutes.

2. Chop tomatoes fine and let stand, in bowl, for about 20 more minutes.

3. Drain tomatoes thoroughly, and place in a 2-quart saucepan with onions and bay leaf. Bring to a boil, then cook, over moderate heat, for 30 minutes, or until thickened. Stir occasionally but more frequently as sauce thickens. Remove from heat, discard bay leaf, and purée mixture in blender or with food mill.

MAKES ABOUT 2 CUPS

SUGO DI CARNE   *North Italy*
MEAT JUICE

This recipe may look frightening at first and the amount of meats and bones may seem ridiculous for such a small yield. Actually, the recipe practically cooks itself, and the result is so unique and exquisite in taste—and also so necessary in the preparation of many Northern Italian dishes—that we strongly recommend it. Of course it has nothing in common with any commercial products such as Bovril or Maggi.

3 ounces prosciutto fat or larding pork, ground
1 4-by-5-inch piece (about 2½ ounces) pork rind, boiled for 10 minutes and drained
2 pounds rump or shank of beef, cut into chunks
1 pound veal muscle, cut into chunks (boneless shank of veal)
3 to 4 pounds cracked beef and veal bones, with marrow
1 ounce dry mushrooms, soaked in tepid water for 20 minutes, squeezed dried, and chopped
2 large yellow onions, coarsely chopped
2 large carrots, coarsely chopped
2 celery ribs, coarsely chopped
1 clove garlic, chopped
2 cloves
1 teaspoon salt
¼ teaspoon freshly ground black pepper
1 cup dry red wine

Bouquet garni: ¼ *teaspoon dried thyme, 1 crushed bay leaf, 6*
   sprigs of parsley, and ¼ *teaspoon dried marjoram*
⅓ *cup flour*
1 cup chopped Polpa al Pomodoro *(Tomato Pulp), page 4, or 1*
   cup canned imported Italian plum tomatoes, drained, with
   seeds removed, and chopped
3 quarts boiling water
Additional salt and freshly ground black pepper to taste

1. Preheat oven to 300° F.
2. Line bottom of roasting pan with prosciutto fat or larding pork. On top place the pork rind, beef rump or shank, veal muscle, beef and veal bones with marrow, mushrooms, onions, carrots, celery, garlic, cloves, ½ teaspoon salt, and the black pepper. Cook over low heat, stirring occasionally. As soon as meat starts to brown add the wine and bouquet garni. Cook, stirring, until wine is almost evaporated. Remove from heat, sprinkle with flour, and stir well. Return to heat and cook, stirring constantly over very low heat for 1 minute. Add Tomato Pulp or canned tomatoes and mix well. Add boiling water to cover and remaining ½ teaspoon salt. Simmer (do not boil) for 5 minutes. Scum will start to rise. Remove it with spoon or ladle until it ceases to accumulate.
3. Place in oven, partially covered, so that steam may escape, and cook for 4 hours, being very careful that it barely simmers.
4. Take out of oven, remove beef, veal, and pork rind, and reserve for other uses. Strain liquid, discarding vegetables, bones, and bouquet garni, into a saucepan. Simmer until liquid is reduced to 1½ quarts, removing fat from surface with spoon or ladle. Place juice in refrigerator, uncovered, until remaining fat has hardened on top and can be scraped off. Taste for seasoning, and, if flavor is weak, boil to reduce water content further and remove scum if it rises to surface. Meat Juice may be kept in refrigerator or freezer. If kept in the refrigerator, it must be removed and brought to a boil every 3 or 4 days before storing again.

MAKES ABOUT 1 QUART

SALSA AL MARSALA
MARSALA SAUCE

North Italy

2½ *cups Sugo di Carne (Meat Juice), page 8*
½ *cup dry Marsala wine*
2 *tablespoons sweet butter*

Strain Meat Juice, and bring to a boil over high heat, reducing it by one-third. Dilute with Marsala and place in top of a double boiler. Mix in the butter bit by bit and cook, stirring with a wire whisk, until butter is melted and sauce is smooth and creamy.

MAKES ABOUT 2 CUPS

SALSA ALLA BOLOGNESE
BOLOGNESE SAUCE

Emilia-Romagna

Bolognese Sauce is a meat sauce with mushrooms which originated in Bologna. It may be served with any pasta, rice, polenta, or gnocchi, and as an ingredient in other dishes as directed in recipes.

3 *tablespoons sweet butter*
about 2 ounces lean prosciutto or lean salt pork, diced
½ *cup chopped yellow onions*
⅓ *cup grated carrots*
⅓ *cup chopped celery*
1 *pound mixed beef, pork and veal, in equal amounts, and ground together*
1 *ounce dry mushrooms, soaked in tepid water for 20 minutes, squeezed dry, and chopped*
1½ *cups dry red wine*
1 *tablespoon chopped fresh parsley*

1 teaspoon dried marjoram
1 teaspoon salt
½ teaspoon freshly ground black pepper
¼ teaspoon freshly grated or ground nutmeg
1½ teaspoons flour
3 cups chopped Polpa al Pomodoro *(Tomato Pulp), page 4, or*
    3 cups canned imported Italian plum tomatoes, drained, with
    seeds removed, and chopped
2 cups Brodo di Manzo *(Beef Broth), page 36*
½ cup heavy cream (optional)

1. Melt butter in saucepan. Add prosciutto or salt pork and sauté over low heat until browned.

2. Add onions, carrots, and celery and cook, over low heat, stirring for about 6 or 7 minutes, or until onions are golden.

3. Add the meat and mushrooms. Cook, stirring, for 2 minutes, over moderate heat. Mix in wine, parsley, marjoram, salt, black pepper, and nutmeg. Stir and cook until wine is almost evaporated.

4. Remove from heat and slowly mix in flour. Replace on heat, cook for brief moment only, then add Tomato Pulp. Continue cooking over low heat for 1 hour, adding Beef Broth from time to time and stirring occasionally. When sauce has almost finished cooking, add heavy cream, if desired.

MAKES ABOUT 5 CUPS

SALSA MAIONESE   *North Italy*
MAYONNAISE

Italians are "puritans" about their mayonnaise. They would never dream of using mustard, sugar, or any spice unless you count salt and pepper spices. All that a superb Italian mayonnaise calls for is *really* good olive oil, egg yolks, and a little vinegar or lemon juice.

3 egg yolks
½ teaspoon salt
¼ teaspoon freshly ground black pepper
1⅓ cups olive oil
2 tablespoons white wine vinegar or lemon juice

1. Place egg yolks into a bowl and add the salt and black pepper. Beat thoroughly with a wire whisk, a hand beater, or an electric beater at high speed.

2. Add the oil, 1 tablespoon at a time, beating thoroughly after each addition, until ½ cup of the oil has been added and the sauce is thick. Then add the remaining oil in larger quantities and, last, the vinegar or lemon juice.

MAKES ABOUT 2 CUPS

NOTE: If oil is added too rapidly, mayonnaise may curdle. If this happens, immediately beat curdled mixture into another egg yolk. Then continue adding rest of oil and then vinegar or lemon juice.

SALSA CITRONETTE   *North Italy*
CITRONETTE SAUCE

1 teaspoon salt
½ teaspoon freshly ground black pepper
½ cup lemon juice
1½ cups olive oil

1. Place salt and black pepper into a clean dry jar. Add slowly, stirring the lemon juice, until well amalgamated.

2. Add olive oil, close jar, and shake well.

MAKES 2 CUPS

NOTE: Shake again before using.

SALSA VERDE   *North Italy*
GREEN SAUCE

This is one of the requisite sauces served with *Bollito Misto* (Mixed Boiled Meats), page 143, but it is also excellent with hot or cold meats and fish.

> *4 anchovy fillets, mashed to a fine paste*
> *½ cup chopped parsley*
> 6 cetriolini sott'aceto *(Italian pickled gherkins)* *
> *1 medium potato, boiled, peeled, and mashed*
> *½ teaspoon finely minced garlic*
> *2 tablespoons grated yellow onion*
> *½ teaspoon salt*
> *½ teaspoon freshly ground black pepper*
> *6 tablespoons olive oil*
> *2 tablespoons white wine vinegar*
> *2 tablespoons lemon juice*

1. Mix together the anchovy, parsley, *cetriolini sott'aceto,* potato, garlic, onion, salt, and black pepper. Stir thoroughly until mixture becomes pasty in consistency.

2. Add olive oil, 1 tablespoon at a time, beating after each addition. Add vinegar and lemon juice and stir.

MAKES 2½ CUPS

---

* If Italian pickled gherkins are not available, sour gherkins may be substituted.

PESTO ALLA GENOVESE   *Liguria*
PESTO, GENOA STYLE

This is the famous sauce or, better, paste made of fresh basil, garlic, cheese, and pignoli, which has been eaten by the Genoese with all sorts of pasta and as flavoring for soups since time immemorial. An anonymous writer who followed Godefroy de Bouillon to the Holy Land during the First Crusade says that "every evening, at dinner time, from a certain part of the camp came a fragrance of garlic and basil. That part of the camp was the Genoese quarters, easily recognizable, simply with the help of the nose."

The Genoese claim that their basil has a far superior flavor to that grown in any other part of Italy and assert that a good pesto can only be made in Genoa. This is certainly an exaggeration, but one thing is positive, for a really good pesto—which is certainly one of the best sauces as yet invented for pasta and as an addition to make the most delicious minestrone in all of Italy—it is necessary to have fresh basil.

½ cup pignoli (pine nuts)
*¼ cup chopped fresh basil ***
2 tablespoons chopped raw spinach leaves
2 teaspoons finely minced garlic
½ rounded cup freshly grated Fiore Sardo cheese or, if available,
    substitute ¼ cup freshly grated Romano cheese and ¼ cup
    *freshly grated Parmesan cheese ****
6 tablespoons butter, softened
½ cup olive oil
¼ teaspoon salt
⅛ teaspoon freshly ground black pepper

1. With a mortar and pestle, mash the pine nuts, fresh basil, spinach, and garlic to a smooth paste.
2. Stir in, slowly, the cheese and the softened butter.

* If fresh basil is unobtainable, use 1 teaspoon dried basil *plus* 1 cup chopped raw spinach leaves, to give the typical green color to the sauce.
** Fiore Sardo or Romano will make the sauce more piquante. Parmesan alone will yield a milder-tasting pesto.

3. Then add the olive oil, little by little. Season with salt and black pepper. This entire "Operation Pesto" can be done in a blender, but mix *all* the ingredients together before blending. If made in larger quantities, pesto may be covered with a layer of olive oil, stored in jars, and placed in the refrigerator.

MAKES 1 CUP

SALSA VINAIGRETTE   *North Italy*
VINAIGRETTE SAUCE

This is our own version of the classic Italian vinaigrette, which does not include mustard, lemon juice, and Tabasco sauce. Our Vinaigrette Sauce may be used as a basic salad dressing.

⅓ cup red wine vinegar
1 teaspoon salt
¼ teaspoon freshly ground black pepper
¼ teaspoon dry mustard
⅔ cup olive oil
1 tablespoon lemon juice
3 drops Tabasco sauce

1. Mix vinegar with salt, black pepper, and mustard.
2. Then add the olive oil, lemon juice, and Tabasco, and stir or shake well.

MAKES ABOUT 1 CUP

SALSA AL CIOCCOLATO   *North Italy*
CHOCOLATE SAUCE

3 ounces bitter chocolate
4 tablespoons sweet butter
1 tablespoon dark rum
1 tablespoon strong Italian coffee (liquid)
1 cup unsifted confectioners' sugar
1 scant cup evaporated milk
½ teaspoon vanilla extract

1. Melt the chocolate and butter in a double boiler together with the rum and coffee.
2. Remove from heat and stir in the sugar alternately with the evaporated milk. Replace double boiler on heat and cook, stirring constantly, until mixture is thick, smooth, and creamy.
3. Remove from heat and stir in vanilla extract.

MAKES ABOUT 1 CUP

ANTIPASTI

ANTIPASTI

Fondi di Carciofi con Carne di Granzevola

Crostini di Ricotta e Salsiccie
Tartine con Formaggio di Gamberetti
Tartine con Formaggio di Tartufi

Fonduta alla Piemontese

Uova in Sorpresa

Antipasto Matrimonio di Mare
Ostriche con Caviale

Prosciutto e Melone
Prosciutto e Miele
Involtini di Prosciutto con Asparagi

Sardine Estive

Stecchi alla Bolognese

Pomodorini Ripieni

FONDI DI CARCIOFI CON CARNE DI GRANZEVOLA

Veneto

ARTICHOKE BOTTOMS STUFFED WITH CRAB MEAT

This antipasto is a delicacy found only in the greatest restaurants in the world. The preparation of the artichoke bottoms (removing everything but the meaty part of the artichoke) is not complicated if you follow our instructions.

8 large artichokes
½ cup lemon juice
¼ cup flour
2 quarts cold water
1½ teaspoons salt
1 7¾-ounce can crab meat
1 cup Salsa Maionese *(Mayonnaise), page 12*
1 tablespoon chopped fresh parsley plus 8 sprigs of parsley
1 tablespoon small unsalted capers

1. Cut the stem off close to the base of the artichoke. Remove all hard outer leaves until you have gone beyond the curve of the heart and the leaf structure falls inward. Cut off leaves just above the heart of the artichoke using a sharp knife or scissors. Scoop out any red leaves and the fuzzy part, leaving only the meaty part, the artichoke bottom. Immediately rub artichoke bottom with lemon juice inside and outside. Drop artichoke bottoms in 1 quart water to which 3 tablespoons lemon juice have been added.

2. Put the flour in a saucepan of enamel, pyrex, stainless steel, or earthenware. Beat in a bit of the cold water to make a smooth paste. Then pour in rest of water, 1 tablespoon lemon juice, and 1½ teaspoons salt. Bring to a boil and simmer for 5 minutes. Drain artichoke bottoms, and add to flour-water-lemon juice mixture. Bring the liquid to a boil and simmer for

35 minutes or until artichoke bottoms are tender. Remove from heat and let them cool in liquid.

3. Pick over crab meat to remove cartilage pieces, and mash with fork. Combine with ½ cup Mayonnaise and the chopped parsley. Then fill artichoke bottoms with crab meat-mayonnaise-parsley mixture, making a little mound on each. Spread tops with remaining ½ cup Mayonnaise and decorate, all around, with capers. Serve on platter decorated with parsley sprigs.

SERVES 4

CROSTINI DI RICOTTA E SALSICCIE   *North Italy*
CHEESE AND SAUSAGE CANAPÉS

The *crostini,* served with a tossed salad, make an excellent luncheon dish. The mixture may be prepared in advance but the bread should, of course, be fried at the last moment. Each slice may be cut in half, and the triangular *crostini* make excellent canapés served with cocktails. As a main course they should be served with a light dry white wine.

>   *½ pound ricotta cheese* *
>   *3 tablespoons cold water*
>   *½ teaspoon salt*
>   *5 tablespoons freshly grated Parmesan cheese*
>   *3 sweet Italian sausages*
>   *¼ cup plus 2 tablespoons olive oil*
>   *¼ cup sweet butter*
>   *12 slices white bread, with crusts removed and slices halved*
>   *3½ ounces Piedmontese fontina or French Gruyère, thinly sliced*
>   *and cut into rectangles the same size as bread*

1. In a bowl mix together the ricotta cheese and cold water. Add salt and Parmesan cheese and mix until smooth and creamy.
2. Prick sausages with a fork and cook in ¼ cup of water in skillet,

over low heat, until water is evaporated. Continue cooking sausages until browned on all sides and thoroughly cooked. Remove from skillet, drain, peel, chop fine, and stir into cheese mixture.

3. Preheat oven to 325° F.

4. Heat oil and butter in large, heavy skillet. Add bread slices and fry on one side only. Remove from skillet, drain on paper towels, and keep hot.

5. Spread the fried sides of the bread with the cheese-sausage mixture, place on well-greased baking pan or cookie sheet and bake in oven for 5 minutes.

6. Remove canapés from oven, top each with fontina or Gruyère cheese. Replace in oven for about a minute, or until top cheese has melted.

MAKES 24 CROSTINI

TARTINE CON FORMAGGIO DI GAMBERETTI   *Veneto*
CHEESE AND SHRIMP PASTE CANAPÉS

¼ pound shrimps, cooked according to Scampi Stufati nel Vermut *(Shrimps Steamed in Vermouth), page 93*
1 cup freshly grated Parmesan cheese
¼ cup sweet butter, softened
¼ teaspoon salt
¼ teaspoon freshly ground white pepper
½ cup heavy cream
1 tablespoon Cognac
12 slices white bread, with crusts removed and slices halved

1. Preheat oven to 350° F.

2. Chop shrimps fine. Add Parmesan cheese, butter, salt, and white pepper, and purée in blender or with mortar and pestle. Add heavy cream and Cognac and mix well.

* Ricotta is a fresh soft Italian cheese, available in most supermarkets. Its texture varies slightly from brand to brand. Some are quite moist and require less water when mixed with Parmesan cheese.

3. Lightly toast the bread on one side only, in broiler. Spread shrimp-cheese mixture on untoasted side. Slice diagonally into triangular halves.

MAKES 24 CANAPÉS

TARTINE CON FORMAGGIO DI TARTUFI   *Piedmont*

CHEESE AND TRUFFLE CANAPÉS

3½ ounces fresh or canned white truffles,* finely chopped
½ cup freshly grated Parmesan cheese
3 tablespoons sweet butter, softened
1 tablespoon Cognac
1 tablespoon heavy cream
¼ teaspoon Quattro Spezie *(Four Spices), page 3*
6 slices white bread, with crusts removed and slices quartered

1. Mix truffles, Parmesan cheese, and softened butter thoroughly until mixture becomes a very smooth paste. Add the Cognac, heavy cream, and Four Spices. Mix well.
2. Toast bread on one side only in broiler or fry in a little butter. Spread truffle-cheese mixture on untoasted side. Slice diagonally into triangular halves.

MAKES 12 TRIANGLES

FONDUTA ALLA PIEMONTESE   *Piedmont*
FONDUE, PIEDMONT STYLE

Fonduta is an apparently simple dish, but don't let it fool you—it is not so easy to secure the proper result. In fact, traditionally the Piedmontese girl had to pass very strict tests in making *fonduta* before she was considered desirable as a future housewife.

---

* Fresh white truffles are often difficult to obtain, and the canned variety may be substituted. If canned white truffles are unavailable, finely chopped white mushrooms may be substituted, but the taste will be very different.

For authentic Fondue, Piedmont Style, good quality Piedmontese fontina cheese must be used, although the sliced white truffle may be omitted.

> *¾ pound Piedmontese fontina cheese, diced*
> *¾ cup plus 1 tablespoon milk or light cream, heated*
> *¼ teaspoon salt*
> *2 egg yolks, lightly beaten*
> *2½ tablespoons sweet butter, softened*
> *1 large fresh or canned truffle, sliced paper thin*
> *16 crostini, made according to directions for* Crostini di Ricotta E Salsiccie *(Cheese and Sausage Canapés), page 20*

1. Combine the fontina cheese, ¾ cup of the milk or light cream, and salt in top of double boiler. Place over hot water and cook, stirring steadily, until cheese melts. Lightly beat egg yolks with the remaining 1 tablespoon of milk or light cream.

2. Gradually beat the egg yolks and the softened butter into the melted cheese and milk, stirring constantly until the *fonduta* is thickened, smooth and shiny. Pour into a hot serving dish and sprinkle with the truffle slices. Serve with *crostini,* which are dipped into the *fonduta.*

SERVES 4

UOVA IN SORPRESA   *Emilia-Romagna*
Eggs Surprise

The preparation of these eggs in which the filling is a rich, creamy liquid of Meat Juice, Marsala wine, butter, and cream requires care and delicacy. We believe that if you follow our instructions attentively, your results will be not only delicious but, as in the literal translation of the title, "Eggs Surprise."

> *12 extra large or jumbo eggs*
> *1 cup plus 2 tablespoons heavy cream*
> *1 cup plus 3 tablespoons* Sugo di Carne *(Meat Juice), page 8*
> *3 tablespoons sweet butter, melted*
> *¼ cup dry Marsala wine*
> *½ teaspoon freshly ground white pepper*
> *¼ teaspoon freshly grated or ground nutmeg*
> *1½ cups flour*
> *½ cup water*
> *6 slices white bread, crusts removed, each slice buttered, quartered, and toasted **

1. Puncture a small hole on the large end of the eggs with a small needle or pin.

2. Make a larger hole on the other end of the eggs, using a fine knitting needle, nutpick, or similar sharp-pointed instrument, being especially careful. The best procedure to follow is to first make a very small opening and then, with the utensil you are using, remove tiny bits of the shell until you have an opening approximately ¼ inch in diameter. Try to avoid making small lateral fissures or cracks.

3. Blow hard through the smaller holes of 9 of the eggs so that the insides of eggs come out through larger holes into a bowl. Set the egg yolks and whites aside and use for other purposes.

4. Repeat process with the 3 remaining eggs. It is this amount only which will be used in the filling. Beat the 3 eggs very lightly.

---

* A more extravagant but excellent variation to accompany the eggs is to use, instead of buttered toasts, thin grissini (Italian bread sticks) wrapped in very thin slices of lean prosciutto.

5. Lightly mix the 3 eggs, heavy cream, Meat Juice, melted butter, Marsala, white pepper, and nutmeg.

6. With a pastry syringe refill eggs through larger holes. During operation stir filling lightly but frequently, as the ingredients tend to separate. Try to avoid making mixture frothy. As each egg is filled, replace in egg carton, pinhole down.

7. Mix together the flour and water and knead into a dough. Roll scant tablespoons of dough into 12 small balls. Pinch part of each ball into a small pointed cone that will just fit into the larger openings of the eggs.

8. Insert point of dough ball into large opening of each egg, then gently flatten dough around top of egg until it is not quite halfway down the egg. Wet your fingers in water and press edges of dough to eggs so that it will adhere firmly. It is very important that the dough sticks firmly at the edges. Replace eggs in carton, dough side up, and let dough dry completely. Do not place the eggs back into the refrigerator.

9. Place eggs, dough side up, into small twelve-cup muffin tin. Since the eggs do not fit perfectly into the muffin-tin cups, line sides of each cup with folded aluminum foil, so that the eggs will not bounce around when cooking.

10. Place muffin tin with eggs on bottom of a large deep pot or roasting pan. Add cold water to pan, being careful not to pour it on top of eggs, until water is just below the dough caps of the eggs.

11. Bring water slowly to a simmer. Turn off heat, cover pan tightly, and let stand for 5 minutes.

12. Carefully remove eggs from muffin tin and place each, dough side down, in egg or demitasse cup with saucers underneath. Serve each with butter knife and small egg or demitasse spoon. Accompany eggs with buttered toast squares.

SERVES 12

ANTIPASTO MATRIMONIO DI MARE   *Veneto*
OYSTER AND SHRIMP APPETIZERS

Since in Italian *ostrica* (oyster) is feminine in gender, and *scampo* (shrimp) is masculine, this combination becomes a marriage of the sea.

> 12 large, fresh oysters, on the half-shell,* or prepared according
>   to instructions below
> 12 small shrimps, prepared as in Scampi Stufati nel Vermut
>   (Shrimps Steamed in Vermouth), page 93
> ½ cup minced celery hearts
> 1½ tablespoons Salsa Citronette (Citronette Sauce), page 12
> 1 recipe Salsa Maionese (Mayonnaise), page 12
> ½ teaspoon dry mustard
> ¼ teaspoon paprika
> 2 tablespoons dry vermouth
> 2 tablespoons heavy cream
> 1 large or 2 small lemons, sliced into thin wedges
> 2 tablespoons minced fresh parsley

1. Scrub the oysters well under cold running water. Hold each oyster firmly with thick part of shell toward palm of hand. Insert a strong, thin knife blade between the valves near the back and run it along until it cuts the strong muscle which holds the shell together. Drop the oysters into a strainer set over a bowl and reserve the liquid that drains through for use in cooking the oysters. Pick over each oyster separately to remove any remaining bits of shell. Discard the upper, or smaller, halves of each shell but save the larger part and scrub inside and out thoroughly.

2. Placed the shucked oysters in a saucepan with their liquor. Bring to a boil quickly and remove from heat immediately. Drain the oysters. Discard liquor.

3. Steam shrimps according to recipe on page 93. Let them cool, then shell and devein.

---

* If possible, ask your local fish store to prepare your oysters "on the half-shell," because oysters, unlike clams, are very difficult to cut open.

4. Dress the minced celery hearts with the Citronette Sauce and make a small bed of them on the bottom half of each oyster shell.

5. Arrange 1 oyster and 1 shrimp on top of each celery-covered half-shell.

6. Mix Mayonnaise with mustard, paprika, vermouth, and cream. Beat well until thoroughly blended.

7. Top oysters and shrimps with a tablespoon or so of the Mayonnaise mixture. Arrange on platter, decorate with lemon wedges, and sprinkle each shell with minced parsley.

SERVES 6

OSTRICHE CON CAVIALE   *Veneto*
OYSTERS WITH CAVIAR

2 dozen fresh oysters on the half-shell,* or prepared according to
    instructions below
2 tablespoons fine quality black caviar
2 tablespoons lemon juice
⅛ teaspoon cayenne pepper
Crushed ice
Sprigs of parsley
2 lemons, thinly sliced and each slice cut in half

1. Scrub oyster shells thoroughly under running water until clean. Hold oyster firmly with thick part of shell toward palm of hand. Insert a strong, thin knife between the shell halves near the back and run it around the shell until it cuts the strong muscle which holds the shell halves together. Rinse deep halves of oyster shells (discard other halves) and oyster meat separately in cold water. Drain and place oyster in deep half of shell.

2. Mix together the caviar, lemon juice, and cayenne pepper, and spread thinly over oysters in half-shell. Arrange oysters on large platter or individual plates filled with crushed ice. Decorate with sprigs of parsley and lemon slices.

SERVES 4 TO 6

* If possible, ask your local fish store to prepare your oysters "on the half-shell," because oysters, unlike clams, are very difficult to cut open.

PROSCIUTTO E MELONE   *Emilia-Romagna*
PROSCIUTTO AND MELON

This antipasto is now popular all over Italy, but I have included it here because the practice of eating prosciutto and melon together originated in Emilia-Romagna. The prosciutto classically and correctly used with melon is the prosciutto from Parma, in the Emilia-Romagna region. If the prosciutto is unobtainable, ham slices—not the packaged or canned variety—may be substituted.

> *1 cantaloupe or honeydew melon, chilled*
> *¼ teaspoon salt*
> *⅛ teaspoon freshly ground black pepper*
> *¼ pound thinly sliced prosciutto*

Cut melon into small wedges and remove seeds. Season lightly with salt and black pepper and serve on individual salad plates, with sliced prosciutto.

SERVES

PROSCUITTO E MIELE   *Tuscany*
PROSCIUTTO AND HONEY CANAPÉS

> *6 slices bread, crusts removed, cut in half*
> *1 small jar honey*
> *12 slices prosciutto or 12 thin slices cured ham, cut the same size*
> *   as the bread slices*

1. Toast bread slices on both sides.
2. Spread each piece of bread lightly with honey and top with 1 slice of prosciutto.

MAKES 12 CANAPÉS

INVOLTINI DI PROSCIUTTO CON ASPARAGI
Lombardy

PROSCIUTTO ROLLS STUFFED WITH ASPARAGUS

This dish can be prepared well ahead of time. Just the final 10 minutes of baking is necessary at the last moment.

48 asparagus stalks (approximately 3 pounds)
3 tablespoons salt
6 quarts boiling water (use an enamel pan)
¾ pound prosciutto, thinly sliced and cut into 12 rectangles, about 3½ inches wide by 8 inches long
¾ cup sweet butter, melted (more, if needed)
1 cup freshly grated Parmesan cheese

1. Break off tough ends of asparagus at the point where it easily bends and breaks—usually about halfway up the stalk. Scrape off the scales below the tip and wash asparagus carefully. The ends may be reserved for other uses. Align the asparagus spears and cut them so that all spears are of equal length. Tie in bunches about 2 inches in diameter. Add the salt to the boiling water, and then add the asparagus bunches. Cook for about 10 minutes, or until tender but firm. Remove bunches, drain and untie.

2. Preheat oven to 350° F.

3. Place small bunches of 4 asparagus tips each on a slice of prosciutto, sprinkle each bunch with 1 teaspoon melted butter and a pinch of Parmesan cheese, wrap the prosciutto around each bunch and secure with toothpick.

4. Place asparagus-prosciutto rolls into well-buttered 4-quart baking dish.

5. Pour remaining butter over the rolls and sprinkle with remaining Parmesan cheese.

6. Bake for 10 minutes, or until cheese is golden. Serve hot.

SERVES 6

SARDINE ESTIVE   *Emilia-Romagna*
SARDINES, SUMMER STYLE

This antipasto is not only handsome and colorful to the eye, but with small crackers, we found it to be a great success when served with cocktails either before dinner or at a cocktail party. It is actually quite easy and quick to prepare.

> *4½ cups finely chopped* Polpa al Pomodoro *(Tomato Pulp)*,
>   *page 4*
> *½ teaspoon finely minced garlic*
> *¼ teaspoon ground sage*
> *1 tablespoon butter*
> *¼ teaspoon salt*
> *2 medium green peppers*
> *2 tablespoons olive oil*
> *¼ teaspoon freshly ground black pepper*
> *3 3¼-ounce cans large, skinless sardines, packed in olive oil*
> *5 hard-boiled eggs, with yolks and whites finely chopped separately*

1. In a heavy saucepan, over low heat, or in a double boiler, cook the Tomato Pulp, garlic, sage, butter, and ⅛ teaspoon salt, stirring, until all ingredients are well mixed. Remove from heat and cool.

2. Spear green peppers with long fork or regular skewer and roast over high flame on all sides until skins are black. Peel off skin under cold water. (An alternative to this part of the preparation of the peppers—although it is not so traditionally Italian—is to cover them with water, bring to a boil, remove from heat, let stand for 10 minutes, drain and skin.)

3. Cut peppers into long slivers, discarding seeds and fibers. Marinate pepper slivers in a combination of the olive oil, ⅛ teaspoon salt, and black pepper for 10 minutes.

4. In the meantime arrange part of the sardines in a fanlike pattern in center of a round platter, then repeat arrangement in an outer circle, but leaving a space of 2 to 2½ inches between the sardines. Spoon tomato

sauce over each sardine. In between the tomato-covered sardines of both circles place small mounds of the chopped hard-boiled eggs, alternating the yolks and the whites. Remove pepper slivers from marinade and border the platter with them.

SERVES 6

STECCHI ALLA BOLOGNESE
SHISH KEBAB, BOLOGNA STYLE

Emilia-Romagna

A sort of Bolognese shish kebab appetizer, with skewered slices of veal, Gruyère cheese, bread chunks, and Bolognese mortadella sausage dipped in batter and deep fried.

¼ cup sweet butter
1 tablespoon olive oil
1½ pounds veal slices, flattened to about ¼-inch thickness
Salt and freshly ground black pepper to taste
1 pound mortadella sausage, cut into 1-inch squares, ½ inch thick
12 slices bread, crusts removed, cut into 1-inch squares
¾ pound imported French Gruyère, cut into 1-inch cubes
1 cup tepid milk
1 cup flour
2 eggs, lightly beaten
2 cups unflavored breadcrumbs
2 cups olive oil or other cooking oil

1. Heat butter in a large frying pan until it is foaming. Add olive oil. Add veal and cook, turning, for about 25 minutes over very low heat, or until veal is tender. (If you are able to obtain really pink baby veal, your cooking time will be less and the results more tender.) Season lightly with salt and pepper.

2. On individual wooden skewers, skewer first a square of mortadella, a square of bread, a cube of Gruyère, another square of bread, a square of veal, a cube of Gruyère, and finish off with another square of mortadella. Repeat this operation on a total of 12 skewers.

3. Dip the skewers in the tepid milk, then in the flour, then in the beaten eggs, and then in the breadcrumbs. Dip them again into the eggs and once more in the breadcrumbs.

4. Heat the oil in a large, deep frying pan. Add skewers and deep fry until the crusts are crisp and golden. Remove from oil, drain on paper towels, and serve.

SERVES 6

POMODORINI RIPIENI   *Emilia-Romagna*
STUFFED CHERRY TOMATOES

Stuffed Cherry Tomatoes may be served as an appetizer with drinks or with a bland fish course. A cold steamed salmon or striped bass could be served surrounded by *Pomodorini*.

1 7-ounce can tuna fish, packed in olive oil
2 teaspoons finely chopped scallions
2 teaspoons finely chopped parsley
¼ cup Salsa Maionese (Mayonnaise), page 12
6 drops Tabasco sauce
*48 cherry tomatoes ***

1. Purée tuna. Add scallions, parsley, Mayonnaise, and Tabasco and mix well.

2. Cut top off each tomato, and with the handle of a fork or spoon remove seeds and water. Place them upside down on a platter so that more water drains out. Stuff each tomato with tuna and Mayonnaise mixture. Serve along with chilled dry white wine.

SERVES 6 TO 8

* When in season, plum tomatoes, halved, may be used. They are tastier than cherry tomatoes but contain more liquid. In order to drain them, they should be salted before they are turned upside down on a platter.

SOUPS

ZUPPE

Brodo Classico
Brodo di Manzo
Brodo di Pollo
Brodo Ristretto

Zuppa Pavese
Ginestrata
Passatelli
Spinaci in Brodo

Minestrone alla Genovese

Risi e Bisi

Zuppa di Funghi
Zuppa di Zucca

Zuppa di Pomodoro con Polpettine di Vitello

Crostoncini per Minestra

BRODO CLASSICO
Classic Broth
North Italy

2 pounds beef chuck
1 2½-pound chicken, with giblets
2 pounds marrow bones
6 quarts cold water
1 large yellow onion, larded with 1 clove
3 medium carrots
3 leeks, roots and green stalks removed
2 ribs of celery
3 fresh tomatoes, quartered
2 bay leaves, crushed
2 tablespoons chopped fresh parsley
1 teaspoon thyme
½ teaspoon finely minced garlic
1 teaspoon salt
3 peppercorns
4 egg whites

1. Place beef, chicken, chicken giblets, and marrow bones in a large 7- to 8-quart kettle. Add 6 quarts cold water and bring slowly to a boil. Remove scum that forms on top of water.

2. Add the onion, carrots, leeks, celery, tomatoes, bay leaves, parsley, thyme, garlic, salt, and peppercorns, and simmer very slowly for 3½ hours. Remove meats and use as desired.

3. Strain broth, and place, uncovered, in refrigerator until all fat has congealed at the top. Remove all fat and strain broth through a cheesecloth.

4. Clarification: With a wire whisk beat 1½ cups broth with the egg whites into a very clean greaseless bowl. Bring rest of broth to a boil in a

clean saucepan. Then, continually beating the egg white mixture, gradually pour the boiling broth into it in a very thin stream. Return mixture to saucepan and set over moderate heat until it barely reaches a simmer, continually stirring it slowly with the wire whisk so that egg whites circulate constantly. As soon as the liquid begins to simmer, stop stirring. The egg whites will mount to the surface. Reduce heat even further, so that liquid no longer simmers, and cook for another 10 minutes.

5. Line a colander with four or five layers of clean, damp cheesecloth and place over a very clean, greaseless bowl. The colander should be of a size that its bottom will not touch the surface of the liquid which is to be poured into the bowl. Very gently ladle the broth and egg whites into the cheesecloth, disturbing the egg whites as little as possible. The liquid will drain through, leaving the egg whites behind. Let egg whites drain undisturbed for 5 minutes before removing colander and discarding egg whites.

MAKES ABOUT 2 QUARTS

BRODO DI MANZO   *North Italy*
BEEF BROTH

For this broth, follow exactly the recipe for *Brodo Classico* (Classic Broth), page 35, but omit the chicken and giblets and increase beef and marrow bones to 3 pounds each.

MAKES ABOUT 2 QUARTS

BRODO DI POLLO   *North Italy*
CHICKEN BROTH

1 3- to 4-pound chicken with giblets, cut into small pieces
2 medium carrots
2 medium leeks, roots and green stems removed
3½ quarts water
1 teaspoon salt
4 egg whites

1. Preheat oven to 350° F.
2. Dry chicken pieces carefully. Chop giblets, carrots, and leeks.
3. Place chicken pieces in preheated oven and bake for 15 to 20 minutes, or until slightly golden.
4. Remove from oven, discard any melted fat, and place in kettle. Add cold water and bring slowly to a simmer. Remove scum as it rises to the top. When scum has ceased to accumulate—after about 5 minutes of simmering—add giblets, carrots, leeks, and salt. Simmer, partially covered (leaving about 1 inch uncovered so that steam may escape), for about 1½ hours. Do not let it boil or fat will be reabsorbed into the broth, making it more cloudy.
5. When cooking process is completed, remove chicken and use as desired. Strain broth, discard vegetables and giblets, and place it, uncovered, in refrigerator until fat has congealed on top and may be removed.
6. Proceed with process of clarification as in Classic Broth, page 35.

MAKES ABOUT 2 QUARTS

BRODO RISTRETTO   *North Italy*
CONSOMMÉ

Consommé is the only soup that may be served with the first course. All other soups take the place of the pasta dish, especially at dinner time. Consommé is never served with Parmesan cheese but often with the addition of a wine such as Madeira, port, or sherry.

The use of the *unpeeled* onion gives a particularly golden color to the consommé. As late as the nineteenth century some recipes for consommé called not for the unpeeled onion but for twenty grains of amber.

2 quarts Brodo Classico *(Classic Broth), page 35*
½ pound lean beef, ground
1 medium yellow onion, washed but unpeeled
4 egg whites

1. Before clarifying this consommé, add ground beef and onion and simmer for about ½ hour.

2. Strain broth to remove ground beef and onion. Degrease, then follow process of clarification as in Classic Broth, using the egg whites. Serve hot or cold.

SERVES 6

ZUPPA PAVESE   *Lombardy*
EGG SOUP

According to tradition this dish was born in 1525, on the day King Francis I of France was defeated by Emperor Charles V of the Holy Roman Empire. The king pronounced the historical phrase "Everything is lost but honor." But there was at least one other thing he hadn't lost—his appetite. He stormed the Pavese countryside, famished, in search of something to eat. Finally he arrived at a farm where a peasant woman was brewing a soup. The king told her who he was and that he was very hungry. The woman placed a piece of old bread in a bowl, covered it with broth and then, thinking that this food was not noble enough for a king, even a defeated one, she went to the henhouse, picked up two eggs and broke them into his soup bowl. Naturally the recipe has grown a bit more sophisticated since then.

6 tablespoons sweet butter
2 tablespoons olive oil
6 thin slices Italian bread, quartered
1½ quarts Brodo Classico (Classic Broth), page 35
6 eggs
¼ teaspoon freshly ground white pepper
1¼ cups freshly grated Parmesan cheese

1. Heat butter and olive oil in skillet and fry bread on both sides until crisp and golden. Remove, drain on paper towels, and keep hot.

2. Bring the Classic Broth to a simmer. Break 1 egg at a time into a shallow dish or saucer, and slide it carefully into the broth. Cook each egg until it is set. Then remove, one by one, to individual hot soup plates. Sprinkle with white pepper.

3. After all eggs are removed, bring the broth to a boil again, and strain through a cheesecloth-lined colander. Then pour the strained broth over the eggs. Arrange the bread around the eggs, and sprinkle with ¼ cup of the Parmesan cheese. Serve with remaining Parmesan cheese in a separate bowl.

SERVES 6

GINESTRATA   *Tuscany*
EGG AND MARSALA SOUP

6 egg yolks
½ cup dry Marsala wine
3 cups Brodo di Pollo *(Chicken Broth)*, page 36
¼ teaspoon cinnamon
4 tablespoons sweet butter, softened
¼ teaspoon sugar
¼ teaspoon nutmeg

1. Beat the egg yolks in a large bowl, and, bit by bit, stirring, add the Marsala, the Chicken Broth, and the cinnamon.
2. Place mixture in double boiler. Cook over moderate heat, adding the butter very slowly. When the soup starts to thicken, remove it from heat.
3. Combine the sugar and the nutmeg and sprinkle on surface of soup. Serve in preheated individual bowls.

SERVES 3 TO 4

PASSATELLI   *Emilia-Romagna*
Soup with Egg and Cheese Strip Dumplings

1½ quarts Brodo Classico *(Classic Broth)*, *page 35*
3 eggs plus 1 egg yolk
1¾ cups freshly grated Parmesan cheese
¾ cup unflavored breadcrumbs
2 tablespoons beef marrow or 2 tablespoons sweet butter, softened.*
¼ teaspoon freshly grated or ground nutmeg
¼ teaspoon salt
⅛ teaspoon freshly ground black pepper

1. Bring the Classic Broth to a boil.

2. Meanwhile, mix the eggs, egg yolk, ¾ cup of the Parmesan cheese, breadcrumbs, softened butter or beef marrow, nutmeg, salt, and black pepper thoroughly into a paste. Put the paste into a potato ricer, hold it over the bubbling broth and push paste through so that it falls into the broth in the form of 2-inch-long pieces the size of large spaghetti.

3. Reduce heat until broth is only simmering and cook for 2 minutes. Serve immediately with a bowl of the remaining 1 cup Parmesan cheese.

Serves 6

---

* In Romagna beef marrow is substituted for butter.

SPINACI IN BRODO
SPINACH AND EGG SOUP

Emilia-Romagna

5 tablespoons sweet butter
2 pounds fresh spinach or 2 10-ounce packages frozen spinach, cooked, drained, and finely chopped
1½ teaspoons salt
¼ teaspoon freshly ground white pepper
¼ teaspoon freshly grated or ground nutmeg
3 eggs
½ cup freshly grated Parmesan cheese
1½ quarts Brodo Classico *(Classic Broth)*, *page 35*
1 recipe Crostoncini per Minestra *(Croutons for Soups)*, *page 47*

1. Melt the butter in a saucepan. Add the cooked spinach, salt, white pepper, and nutmeg. Cook over low heat for 3 minutes, stirring constantly. Remove from heat and let it cool completely.

2. Preheat oven to 350° F.

3. Beat the eggs and Parmesan cheese together, then add the spinach.

4. Bring the Classic Broth to a boil, and add the spinach-egg-cheese mixture. Remove immediately from heat.

5. Cover and place soup in oven. Cook for about 20 minutes or until eggs and spinach have coagulated into a green crust on top. Serve with Croutons for Soups.

SERVES 6

MINESTRONE ALLA GENOVESE   *Liguria*
MINESTRONE, GENOA STYLE

It is the addition of the pesto—the fresh basil and cheese paste—that makes this minestrone one of the most unique in all of Italy.

4 tablespoons olive oil

2 ounces lean salt pork, chopped

3 cups Fagioli al Vino Rosso *(Kidney Beans Cooked in Red Wine), page 151*

4 tightly packed cups shredded or coarsely chopped raw spinach

1 cup peeled and diced potatoes

1 cup shredded cabbage

1 leek, with bottom and green stalks removed; remaining white part thinly sliced

2 medium yellow onions, chopped

2 quarts water (use water in which the beans have been cooked, supplemented with fresh water)

2 teaspoons salt

½ teaspoon freshly ground black pepper

1½ cups uncooked linguini, broken into 1-inch pieces

½ cup Pesto alla Genovese *(Pesto, Genoa Style), page 14*

1. Heat the 4 tablespoons olive oil in large, heavy pot, then sauté the salt pork in the oil for about 2 minutes. Add the Kidney Beans, spinach, potatoes, cabbage, leek, and onions, and sauté for 4 to 5 minutes, stirring constantly.

2. Add the 2 quarts of water, salt, and black pepper. Bring to a boil, then reduce to low heat and cook, uncovered, for 1 hour. If liquid reduces too fast, add more boiling water.

3. Add the linguini and cook 15 minutes longer, stirring occasionally. Remove soup from heat, add the Pesto, Genoa Style, let stand for 2 minutes, then stir well, and serve.

SERVES 6

RISI E BISI   *Veneto*
RICE AND PEA SOUP

On April 25, the day of Saint Mark the Evangelist, patron saint of the Venetian Republic, this soup was offered with much pomp to the doge, because the peas represented the arrival of spring and the rice the bonanza offered by the return of warm weather.

6 tablespoons sweet butter
5 ounces lean prosciutto, chopped
1 medium yellow onion, finely chopped
1 tablespoon chopped fresh parsley
1½ cups uncooked long grain rice
½ cup dry white wine
2 cups shelled, fresh small green peas
6½ cups hot Brodo Classico *(Classic Broth), page 35*
1½ teaspoons salt
¼ teaspoon freshly ground black pepper
1 cup freshly grated Parmesan cheese

1. Melt 4 tablespoons of the butter in a heavy saucepan. Add the chopped prosciutto, onion, and parsley, and cook for 5 minutes, over very low heat, stirring constantly. Add the rice and cook until opaque.

2. Add the wine and cook, over low heat, stirring for about 2 minutes. Add the peas, 2 cups of Classic Broth, salt, and black pepper. Cover, bring to a boil, and cook over low heat, stirring occasionally with a fork, until the broth is absorbed.

3. Add 1 more cup of Classic Broth. When this is absorbed, add the remaining broth and cook until the rice and peas are tender. The entire process of cooking, after the rice and peas are added, should take approximately 18 to 20 minutes.

4. Stir in the Parmesan cheese, the remaining 2 tablespoons butter, and serve immediately.

SERVES 6

ZUPPA DI FUNGHI   *Piedmont*
MUSHROOM SOUP

5 tablespoons sweet butter
1½ pounds fresh mushrooms, cleaned, and finely chopped
½ cup dry Marsala wine
½ cup chopped fresh parsley
½ teaspoon salt
¼ teaspoon freshly ground white pepper
⅛ teaspoon freshly grated or ground nutmeg
4 cups Salsa Besciamella *(Béchamel Sauce)*, *page 3*
1½ cups Brodo di Pollo *(Chicken Broth)*, *page 36*
½ cup light cream

1. Melt butter in large saucepan, and add the mushrooms and sauté, over very low heat, for about 4 to 5 minutes.

2. Stir in the Marsala, parsley, salt, white pepper, and nutmeg. Cook, stirring for 2 minutes, over moderate heat.

3. Add the Béchamel Sauce, and remove from heat. Then add the Chicken Broth and place back on heat. Bring to a boil over moderate heat. When the soup starts to thicken, remove from heat. Stir in the cream and serve immediately.

SERVES 6 TO 8

ZUPPA DI ZUCCA   *Lombardy*
PUMPKIN SOUP

3 *medium leeks, roots and green stalks removed, remaining white*
   parts finely chopped
½ *cup plus 2 tablespoons sweet butter*
1⅓ *cups cooked fresh pumpkin pulp or 1 10-ounce can pumpkin*
   pulp
3 *large potatoes, skinned and thinly sliced*
Bouquet garni: ½ *teaspoon dried thyme, 1 tablespoon chopped*
   fresh parsley, and 1 bay leaf, crushed
1 *quart* Brodo di Pollo *(Chicken Broth), page 36*
1½ *teaspoons salt*
½ *teaspoon freshly ground black pepper*
⅛ *teaspoon freshly grated or ground nutmeg*
3 *cups hot milk*
½ *pound fresh spinach, cleaned and chopped*
¼ *teaspoon sugar*
½ *cup freshly grated Parmesan cheese*

1. In a large heavy pan or casserole sauté the chopped leeks in 4 table-spoons butter until golden.

2. Add the pumpkin pulp, sliced potatoes, bouquet garni, 3 cups of the Chicken Broth, salt, black pepper, and nutmeg. Mix well. Bring to a boil, then cook, over very moderate heat, for ½ hour, stirring frequently.

3. Remove the bouquet garni and purée the leek-pumpkin-potato mixture in blender. Return to pan, add the hot milk, and bring to a boil. Reduce the heat to low and cook for 20 minutes, stirring frequently.

4. Meanwhile, cook and thoroughly drain the chopped spinach. Melt 2 tablespoons butter in a skillet, and sauté the spinach in it for 2 minutes more, over low heat.

5. When the pumpkin mixture has finished cooking add the spinach, the remaining 1 cup Chicken Broth, and the sugar. Mix well. Remove from heat. Add the remaining 4 tablespoons butter and Parmesan cheese, and mix.

SERVES 6 TO 8

ZUPPA DI POMODORO CON POLPETTINE DI VITELLO

Marche-Umbria

TOMATO SOUP WITH VEAL DUMPLINGS

4 medium potatoes, peeled and sliced
5 cups chopped Polpa al Pomodoro *(Tomato Pulp)*, page 4
¼ pound prosciutto, chopped
½ cup chopped yellow onion
¼ cup chopped carrots
¼ cup chopped celery
½ teaspoon finely minced garlic
2 tablespoons chopped fresh parsley
1½ teaspoons salt
½ teaspoon freshly ground black pepper
5 to 5½ cups Brodo Classico *(Classic Broth)*, page 35
1 tablespoon sweet butter
½ pound ground lean veal
2 egg yolks
2 slices white bread, crusts removed, dipped in milk, squeezed dry
 and mashed
2 tablespoons freshly grated Parmesan cheese
⅛ teaspoon freshly grated or ground nutmeg

1. Place the potatoes, Tomato Pulp, chopped prosciutto, ¼ cup onion, carrots, celery, garlic, parsley, 1 teaspoon salt, ¼ teaspoon black pepper, and 1 cup of Classic Broth into a kettle. Bring to a boil and cook over moderate heat for 1½ hours, stirring occasionally. If mixture gets too thick, add a bit more broth.

2. Meanwhile, melt butter in a small saucepan, add the remaining ¼ cup chopped onion, and sauté over very low heat, until onion is golden but not soft. Remove from heat and place into a bowl together with the ground veal, egg yolks, bread, Parmesan cheese, ½ teaspoon salt, ¼ teaspoon pepper, and the nutmeg. Mix together thoroughly and form into walnut-sized balls.

3. Bring the 4 cups of remaining Classic Broth to a boil, and drop the veal dumplings into it. Reduce the heat immediately and cook, over low heat, for 20 minutes.

4. When the Tomato Soup has finished cooking, put through a food mill or blender, then add it to the veal dumplings and broth. Mix well, being careful not to break the veal dumplings. Add more broth if soup is too thick.

SERVES 6 TO 8

CROSTONCINI PER MINESTRA   *North Italy*
CROUTONS FOR SOUPS

4 tablespoons.sweet butter
2 tablespoons olive oil
6 slices white bread, crusts removed, and bread cubed

1. Heat butter and oil in skillet, and sauté bread cubes, tossing with a spoon, until they are crisp and golden on all sides.

2. Remove bread cubes and drain on paper towels. Add to soup just before serving.

SERVES 6 AS GARNISH FOR SOUPS

PASTA

PASTA

Pasta all'Uovo
Pasta Verde

Agnolotti con Sugo di Carne

Cannelloni

Lasagne Pasticciata con Prosciutto e Funghi
Lasagne Verdi al Forno

Timballo di Maccheroncelli alla Ferrarese

Spaghetti con Melanzane
Spaghetti con Tonno e Acciughe

Tagliatelle con le Noci
Tagliatelle Verdi con Animèlle e Salsiccie alla Genovese
Tagliolini Freddi

Tortellini in Brodo

Gnocchi

Strozzapreti alla Fiorentina

Sardenaira

PASTA ALL'UOVO *Predominantly North Italy*
EGG PASTA

The following recipe is the basic one for egg pasta. After the dough is made, it may then be used in the preparation of a number of dishes, such as *tagliatelle*, tortellini, ravioli, and *agnolotti*, according to the way in which the dough is cut.

Believe it or not, making fresh egg pasta is not a complicated or difficult process, but it does take time, patience, and physical endurance. Fresh egg pasta is truly superior to the commercial varieties available. However, our recommendation is: BUY AN ITALIAN PASTA MACHINE! It fragments the amount of time needed, it reduces the physical labor to almost nil, it costs only $25 to $30, and it's *fun* to use.

> *5 cups flour*
> *1 teaspoon salt*
> *5 eggs, lightly beaten*
> *1 tablespoon olive oil*

1. Sift the flour onto a board and make a well or depression in the center.

2. Put the salt, lightly beaten eggs, and oil into the well, and work them with your fingers into the flour until you have a firm dough. Continue kneading for about 20 minutes, or until dough is smooth and elastic. During the kneading, flour your hands and the board frequently.

3. Divide dough into two or three parts. Roll out each part, one at a time, on a large floured surface (you will need one of those extra long Italian rolling pins). After first rolling each part, wrap it around the rolling pin, and stretch it a bit. Roll out again, sprinkle with flour, roll over pin again, stretch a little more and repeat process at least ten times for each part of dough, until all pieces are very thin, smooth, and greatly enlarged.

4. Then roll each part two or three more times until it is thin enough to see the graining of the rolling surface through it, but dry enough to pick up like a piece of material. As each piece of dough has been thoroughly rolled, place over the back of a chair or clean cloth before proceeding with the next piece. When all of the pasta is rolled out, dry it for about 30 minutes. It is now ready for cutting and cooking in any number of ways.

PASTA VERDE   *North Italy*
GREEN EGG PASTA

5 cups flour
2 eggs, lightly beaten
1½ cups purée of cooked, fresh spinach, or 2 10-ounce boxes
    frozen spinach, thoroughly drained and puréed *

1. Sift the flour onto a board and make a well or depression in the center.

2. Put eggs and spinach purée into well and work the ingredients together with your fingers until you have a firm dough. Continue kneading for about 20 minutes, or until dough is smooth and elastic. Flour your hands and the board frequently. Then follow instructions for rolling out dough as in *Pasta all'Uovo* (Eggs Pasta), page 51. *Paste Verde* (Green Egg Pasta) is then ready for cutting and cooking in any number of ways.

* It is important that the spinach be as dry as possible; otherwise, you'll have to use much more flour for kneading and rolling the dough and you'll end up with a great quantity of very floury tasting pasta, rather deprived of the spinach flavor.

AGNOLOTTI CON SUGO DI CARNE *Piedmont*
Stuffed "Round Ravioli" with Meat Juice

Agnolotti, or, in regional dialect, agnulot, is the Piedmontese version of ravioli but they are larger in shape and are round instead of square. When prepared and ready to be cooked they remind you of a priest's hat. As in many other cases of stuffed egg pasta, such as tortellini and cappelletti (Emilia-Romagna specialties), *agnolotti* are reserved for Italian winter festivities, such as Christmas, New Year's Eve, and Twelfth Night. This version, with the use of Meat Juice, though elaborate to prepare, is a particularly good one, both rich and delicate, and unusual for the American public.

> ½ cup plus 2 tablespoons sweet butter
> 1 medium yellow onion, chopped
> ¼ pounds prosciutto * or ham
> ¾ pound ground lean veal
> 1 cup dry white wine
> 1 tablespoon flour plus 3 cups sifted flour
> 3 cups Sugo di Carne (Meat Juice), page 8
> ¼ teaspoon freshly ground black pepper
> ¼ teaspoon freshly grated or ground nutmeg
> 3 cups freshly grated Parmesan cheese
> 3 large eggs, lightly beaten
> 1½ tablespoons olive oil
> 3 quarts boiling water or a mixture of Brodo di Pollo (Chicken Broth), page 35, and water
> 1½ tablespoons salt

1. Melt 4 tablespoons butter in a heavy frying pan. Add onion and prosciutto or ham and sauté, stirring frequently, until onion is golden. Add ground veal, mix thoroughly, and cook, stirring, for 1 more minute.

---

* It is very important that a sweet, not too salty, prosciutto be used. Otherwise, ham definitely should be substituted or the *agnolotti* stuffing will be too salty. We therefore recommend an American-produced prosciutto called Volpe.

2. Add dry white wine and cook until almost completely evaporated.

3. Add 1 tablespoon flour slowly, stirring so it doesn't lump. Then add ½ cup Meat Juice, black pepper, and nutmeg, and continue stirring and cooking until mixture is thickened.

4. Remove from heat and mix in ½ cup Parmesan cheese. Let cool completely.

5. Mix together sifted flour, lightly beaten eggs, and olive oil. Knead thoroughly, then follow directions for preparation of Egg Pasta, page 51.

6. Cut sheets of dough into strips 2½ to 3 inches wide. Do not let dough get too dry. If necessary, cover with lightly dampened towels.

7. On alternate sheets place heaping teaspoons of meat and cheese mixture at intervals of 2 inches on all sides. Cover with second sheets of dough and press around the little mounds with your fingers. If necessary, moisten fingers to make top and bottom layers of dough adhere. Cut around each mound with a 2½-inch circular cookie cutter (or any other sharp circular instrument), making sure that edges are well sealed.

8. Place *agnolotti* in a single layer on a *very* well-floured board or floured sheets of wax paper. Be very careful that they do not touch each other, or they will stick together.

9. Carefully plunge the *agnolotti* into the salted boiling water or Chicken Broth and water. Cook for about 6 minutes, then remove carefully with a slotted spoon to a colander.

10. Place one layer of *agnolotti* in heated deep serving platter or casserole. Pour ¼ cup Meat Juice over layer, dot with slivers of 1 tablespoon butter, and sprinkle with ¼ cup Parmesan cheese. Repeat operation until all *agnolotti* are used up. You should have about six layers.

11. Serve with remaining Meat Juice in a gravy boat and with a bowl of remaining Parmesan cheese separately.

SERVES 6

CANNELLONI   *North Italy*
CANNELLONI

¾ cup sweet butter
⅔ cup finely chopped yellow onion
⅔ cup finely chopped carrots
⅔ cup finely chopped celery
3 tablespoons finely chopped fresh parsley
1¼ pounds ground prime beef
3 ounces lean prosciutto, chopped
2 ounces dry mushrooms, soaked in tepid water for 20 minutes,
   squeezed dry, and finely chopped
2 tablespoons chopped fresh or canned white truffles (optional)
1 teaspoon salt
½ teaspoon freshly ground black pepper
¼ teaspoon freshly grated or ground nutmeg
2 cups dry white wine
2 tablespoons flour plus 2 cups sifted flour
1 cup chopped Polpa al Pomodoro *(Tomato Pulp), page 4*
3 cups Sugo di Carne *(Meat Juice), page 8*
2 large eggs, lightly beaten
1½ tablespoons olive oil
1¾ cups freshly grated Parmesan cheese
8 quarts boiling water
2½ tablespoons salt

1. Melt ½ cup butter in saucepan. Add chopped onion, carrots, celery, and parsley, and sauté, over very low heat, until onion is golden. Add ground beef and cook, stirring, over moderate heat, for 2 to 3 minutes. Add chopped prosciutto, mushrooms, truffles (if used), and season with salt, black pepper, and nutmeg. Mix well. Add dry white wine, and cook until it has completely reduced.

2. Sprinkle with 2 tablespoons flour, mix well, and add Tomato Pulp and ½ cup Meat Juice. Cook, over moderate heat, until thickened to a pasty consistency, stirring frequently. Remove from heat, and let it cool completely.

3. Mix together 2 cups sifted flour, lightly beaten eggs, and olive oil. Knead thoroughly, then follow directions for preparation of Egg Pasta, page 51. Cut sheets of dough into 3- by 4-inch rectangles. Cook six at a time in boiling salted water for 5 minutes. Remove one at a time with slotted spoon and place unfolded on damp towels. Continue operation until all squares are cooked.

4. Preheat oven to 375° F.

5. Spread about 2 tablespoons of beef mixture on half of each rectangle, across the width, leaving a ½-inch margin at one end. Starting from the spread end of the rectangles, roll each one tightly. Make a layer of the stuffed cannelloni in a large, rectangular, buttered baking pan. Pour 1½ cups of Meat Juice over them, sprinkle with ¾ cup of Parmesan cheese, and dot with remaining butter. If necessary, two layers instead of one can be made, in which case pour half of the Meat Juice, sprinkle with half of the cheese, and dot with half of the butter. Bake uncovered for 15 to 20 minutes. Serve immediately, with remaining Meat Juice in gravy boat and with remaining Parmesan cheese in a bowl.

SERVES 6 TO 8

NOTE: The cannelloni, which can turn out as delicate as *crêpes farcies*, can be prepared ahead of time—even the day before—but in such cases the baking time in the oven must be slightly increased.

LASAGNE PASTICCIATA CON PROSCIUTTO E FUNGHI
Marche-Umbria
BAKED LASAGNE WITH PROSCIUTTO AND MUSHROOMS

½ cup plus 2 tablespoons sweet butter
2 medium yellow onions, chopped
½ cup grated carrots
½ cup chopped celery
2 tablespoons chopped fresh parsley
1 pound ground beef
1-pound ground veal
1 teaspoon salt

¼ teaspoon freshly ground black pepper
¾ pound fresh mushrooms, finely chopped
1½ cups chopped Polpa al Pomodoro (Tomato Pulp), page 4
1½ cups Brodo Classico (Classic Broth), page 35
2 cups flour
2 eggs
1 tablespoon olive oil
8 quarts boiling water
2½ tablespoons salt
½ pound prosciutto, finely shredded
1¾ cups freshly grated Parmesan cheese

1. Melt 4 tablespoons butter in large heavy frying pan or casserole. Add the onions, carrots, celery, and parsley, and sauté lightly until onions are golden.

2. Add the ground beef and veal, salt and black pepper, and cook, stirring, on moderate heat for 15 minutes, or until meats are browned.

3. Add mushrooms and cook, stirring, for 5 minutes. Add Tomato Pulp and Classic Broth, and cook for 30 minutes, uncovered, stirring occasionally. Remove from heat and set aside.

4. Mix together the flour, eggs, and olive oil, and follow the procedure for making Egg Pasta, page 51. Prepare the Egg Pasta, rolled out to a thickness a little thinner than commercial lasagne. Cut the uncooked Egg Pasta into about 4-inch squares. Plunge 6 to 8 pasta squares into boiling salted water. As soon as pasta squares rise to the top, let them cook for about 2 or 3 more minutes. Remove from water one at a time with a slotted spoon and place, unfolded, on thick towels. Dry well and line bottom of a well-buttered deep rectangular or square pan or casserole. (Use the remaining cooked pasta squares to make a second layer.) Cover the pasta with a layer of the meat-mushroom sauce. Sprinkle with 2 tablespoons shredded prosciutto and 1 tablespoon Parmesan cheese, then dot with 1 tablespoon butter.

5. Repeat process of boiling only enough pasta squares at a time to make one or two layers (it always depends on the pan or casserole you use), draining, adding to casserole, and topping with sauce, shredded prosciutto, Parmesan cheese, and butter. Top with final layer of pasta, sprinkle with Parmesan cheese, dot with remaining butter, and place in oven for 15 to 20 minutes at 350° F., or until top is golden and edges of pasta crisp and curly. Remove and serve with a bowl of remaining Parmesan cheese.

SERVES 6 TO 8

NOTE: This recipe for lasagne, like the one that follows, can be prepared well ahead of time, but in that case the baking time in the oven must be increased in order to heat thoroughly the lasagne.

If you use commercial lasagne, follow the instructions for time of cooking on the box, and cook them all at the same time. But, as soon as you remove from water, toss with butter, so that they will not stick together, and you'll easily make the layers.

LASAGNE VERDI AL FORNO   *Emilia-Romagna*
BAKED GREEN LASAGNE

Baked Green Lasagne is not something you are likely to find in Italian restaurants in America. Not only is the green lasagne commercially unavailable, but the addition of the chicken livers and Béchamel Sauce—typically Bolognese—gives a delicate, rich, and unique flavor.

> *5 cups* Salsa alla Bolognese *(Bolognese Sauce), page 10*
> *3 cups* Salsa Besciamella *(Béchamel Sauce), page 3*
> *3 cups freshly grated Parmesan cheese*
> *1 recipe* Pasta Verde *(Green Egg Pasta), page 52*
> *½ cup sweet butter*
> *½ pound chicken livers*
> *8 quarts of boiling water*
> *2½ tablespoons salt*

1. Prepare the Bolognese Sauce, since it takes the longest time. After the Tomato Pulp has been added to the Bolognese Sauce begin to prepare the Béchamel Sauce. When the Béchamel Sauce has finished cooking, mix in ½ cup Parmesan cheese. Mix well, set aside, and keep warm.

2. Prepare the Green Egg Pasta, rolled out to a thickness a little thinner than commercial white lasagne.

3. Melt 2 tablespoons butter in small saucepan. Add the chicken livers and sauté for 1 or 2 minutes or until tan. Chop the livers fine and mix into the Bolognese Sauce, *only* when it has finished cooking.

4. Preheat oven to 375° F.

5. Cut the uncooked green pasta into 4-inch squares. Add 2 tablespoons butter to the boiling salted water (the butter prevents the pasta squares from sticking to each other). Plunge 6 to 8 pasta squares into boiling salted water. As soon as pasta squares rise to the top, cook for about 2 more minutes. Remove from water one at a time with slotted spoon and place, unfolded, on thick towels. Dry well and line bottom of well-buttered deep rectangular or square pan or casserole. Cover the pasta with a layer of the hot Bolognese Sauce, then spread with a thin layer of Béchamel Sauce. Dot sparsely with butter and sprinkle with Parmesan cheese. Repeat process of boiling only enough pasta squares at a time to make one layer, draining, adding to casserole, and topping with sauces, butter, and cheese as before, until sauces are used up. Top with final layer of pasta, sprinkle with Parmesan cheese, dot with remaining butter, and place in oven for 15 to 20 minutes, or until top is golden and edges crisp. Remove and serve with a bowl of remaining Parmesan cheese.

SERVES 8

NOTE: Baked Green Lasagne may be prepared as much as a day ahead, but in that case the baking time in the oven must be increased to thoroughly heat the lasagne.

TIMBALLO DI MACCHERONCELLI   *Emilia-Romagna*
ALLA FERRARESE
Timbale of Miniature Macaroni, Ferrara Style

This dish may seem too elaborate and expensive to prepare in order to get in the end only a pasta dish. But it is so traditionally Italian that we felt it should be included in this book. It is meant to make a pasta dish—a food for centuries reserved for the poor—into a dish rich enough for gourmets. A Southern version of this dish—an even more elaborate concoction of ingredients, sweet and salty (typically Southern)—appears in both the book and the Visconti-directed movie version of the *Leopard*, on the sumptuous table of Principe di Salina during the dinner he gave for his future niece, the bourgeois but ravishing daughter of the merchant, who is to marry his nephew Tancredi.

> 3 tablespoons olive oil
> ¼ cup plus 1 tablespoon sweet butter
> 2 2-ounce slices prosciutto fat or fat salt pork, chopped
> 1 3-pound roasting chicken
> 1 medium yellow onion, coarsely chopped
> ½ cup coarsely chopped carrots
> ½ cup coarsely chopped celery
> ½ teaspoon salt
> ¼ teaspoon freshly ground black pepper
> ½ cup dry white wine
> 1 cup Brodo di Pollo (Chicken Broth), page 36
> 1½ ounces dry mushrooms, soaked in tepid water for 20 minutes, drained, squeezed dry, and chopped
> ½ pound chicken livers, coarsely chopped
> ½ pound maccheroncelli (miniature macaroni)
> 3 quarts boiling water
> 1 tablespoon salt
> 2 cups Salsa Besciamella (Béchamel Sauce), page 3
> ½ pound lean prosciutto or ham, sliced julienne
> ¼ cup plus 1 tablespoon heavy cream
> 1 egg, beaten with 2 tablespoons water
> 4 semibaked bottom pie crusts, according to instructions for

Agnello Brasato in Crosta *(Braised Leg of Baby Lamb Baked in Crust)*, *page 128*
2 cups Parmesan cheese

1. Preheat oven to 350° F.
2. Heat the olive oil, 2 tablespoons butter, and prosciutto fat or fat salt pork, in large, heavy skillet. Add the chicken, onion, carrots, celery, salt, and black pepper, and sauté until chicken is brown on all sides. Add the dry white wine, and cook, over moderate heat, for about 5 minutes, or until wine is almost completely reduced. Continue to turn chicken and vegetables occasionally.
3. Add ¾ cup Chicken Broth and place chicken in oven. Roast for about 1½ hours, or until chicken is tender. Baste frequently, adding more Chicken Broth if needed.
4. When chicken is done, remove from oven, let cook in pan juices until it can be handled without burning your fingers. Leave oven on at 350° F. for later use.
5. Remove chicken from pan juices. Remove skin and chop fine. Bone and slice chicken, julienne style.
6. Scrape bottom and sides of pan. Strain pan juices and return 3 tablespoons to pan. Add 1 tablespoon butter, melt, then add chopped mushrooms and cook for 1 minute over moderate heat, stirring. Add chopped chicken livers and cook for 1 to 2 minutes longer, stirring, or just until the pink of the livers turns lightly brown. Remove from heat and set aside.
7. Plunge the *maccheroncelli* into boiling salted water and cook for about 12 minutes, or until just *al dente*. Drain and replace in pot or kettle.
8. Add Béchamel Sauce, sliced chicken, chopped chicken skin, mushrooms, and chicken livers, the chopped prosciutto or ham, the heavy cream, and 2 remaining tablespoons of butter to the cooked *maccheroncelli*. Toss these ingredients thoroughly.
9. Remove pie crusts from pans intact, being sure that all bits of crust are removed. Rebutter the pie pans. Replace pie crusts in two of the pans and fill with the *maccheroncelli* mixture until they form mounds. Cover with the two unmolded pie crusts. Brush top crusts with egg and water mixture. Place timbales in oven for about 10 minutes, or until tops are golden. Serve Parmesan cheese in separate bowl at the table.

SERVES 8 TO 10

SPAGHETTI CON MELANZANE　　　　*Emilia-Romagna*
SPAGHETTI WITH EGGPLANT

½ pound eggplant, peeled and sliced, julienne style
1 teaspoon salt
¼ cup plus 2 tablespoons sweet butter
¼ cup finely chopped yellow onion
⅛ teaspoon finely minced garlic
¼ teaspoon freshly ground black pepper
½ cup skinned, cubed Pollo Arrosto *(Roast Chicken)*, page 107
2 ounces lean prosciutto, cubed
2 tablespoons Cognac
1 cup chopped Polpa al Pomodoro *(Tomato Pulp)*, page 4
¼ cup olive oil
¼ pound spaghetti, cooked al dente, *and drained*
2 cups freshly grated Parmesan cheese
¼ pound fresh mozzarella cheese, thinly sliced
2 cups Salsa Bolognese *(Bolognese Sauce)*, page 10

1. Place eggplant strips in bowl with ½ teaspoon salt. Toss and let stand for 30 minutes.
2. Melt 4 tablespoons butter in a saucepan. Add chopped onion, garlic, and black pepper, and sauté, on very low heat, until onion is lightly golden. Mix in cubed chicken and prosciutto. Cook, over very low heat, for 1 to 2 minutes, stirring constantly. Inflame Cognac and add to chicken-prosciutto mixture; cook until it is evaporated. Mix in Tomato Pulp and remaining ½ teaspoon salt. Taste for seasoning. Cook, over moderate heat, for 8 to 10 minutes. Remove from heat and keep hot.
3. Drain eggplant strips and pat dry in a towel. Heat olive oil, add eggplant, and fry until brown and tender.
4. Place hot spaghetti on a heated platter or bowl. Toss with remaining 2 tablespoons butter and sprinkle with ½ cup Parmesan cheese. Top with mozzarella slices. Pour half of the chicken-prosciutto sauce and half of the Bolognese Sauce over it, and top with the fried eggplant strips. Serve with remaining sauces in separate gravy boats and with a bowl of the remaining 1½ cups Parmesan cheese.

SERVES 6 TO 8

SPAGHETTI CON TONNO E ACCIUGHE   *Emilia-Romagna*

SPAGHETTI WITH TUNA AND ANCHOVY SAUCE

2 anchovies, soaked in milk for 10 minutes, drained and puréed
2 tablespoons sweet butter, softened
½ cup olive oil
2½ cups chopped Polpa di Pomodoro *(Tomato Pulp), page 4*
1 teaspoon salt
¼ teaspoon freshly ground black pepper
½ cup tuna fish, flaked
1 pound spaghetti, cooked al dente, *and drained*
2 tablespoons chopped fresh parsley

1. Mix together the puréed anchovies and butter and set aside
2. Heat 6 tablespoons olive oil in a saucepan. Add Tomato Pulp, salt, and black pepper, and cook for 15 minutes over moderate heat, stirring occasionally.
3. Heat remaining 2 tablespoons olive oil in a small saucepan. Add tuna and sauté for 2 to 3 minutes on high heat. Remove from heat and keep hot.
4. Place hot spaghetti on a heated platter or bowl. Mix butter-anchovy mixture and tuna with tomato sauce and pour over spaghetti. Sprinkle with chopped parsley.

SERVES 6

TAGLIATELLE CON LE NOCI   *Liguria*
EGG NOODLES WITH WALNUT SAUCE

1 recipe Pasta all'Uovo *(Egg Pasta)*, *page 51*

Walnut sauce:
>   2 tablespoons olive oil
>   2 dozen shelled walnut halves, crushed
>   1 teaspoon salt
>   ½ teaspoon freshly ground black pepper
>   3 tablespoons Purea al Pomodoro (Tomato Purée), page 7
>   ½ cup sweet butter
>   ½ cup Brodo di Pollo (Chicken Broth), page 36

3 quarts boiling water
1 tablespoon salt
1¼ cups freshly grated Parmesan cheese

1. Prepare Egg Pasta.
2. While sheets of pasta are drying, prepare the Walnut Sauce in the following manner: Heat olive oil in small saucepan or skillet. Add crushed walnuts, salt, and black pepper. Sauté, stirring, over low heat, for 2 minutes. Mix in Tomato Purée and butter. Add the Chicken Broth and cook over low heat for 10 minutes, or until reduced and thickened.
3. Bring to a boil 3 quarts of water, and add salt.
4. When the pasta has dried and the sauce is cooking, take each piece of pasta, roll up lightly, like a newspaper, and cut each roll with a sharp knife into strips a little more than ¼ inch wide. Unroll strips and dump into the boiling salted water. As soon as they rise to the top, cook for 5 more minutes, or until tender. Remove, drain thoroughly, and place on hot platter. Add ¼ cup Parmesan cheese and toss lightly.
5. Pour Walnut Sauce over *tagliatelle* and mix until they are well coated. Serve with a bowl of remaining Parmesan cheese.

SERVES 6 TO 8

TAGLIATELLE VERDI CON ANIMÈLLE E SALSICCIE ALLA GENOVESE
GREEN EGG NOODLES WITH SWEETBREADS AND SAUSAGE, GENOA STYLE

Liguria

This pasta is rather unique because the meats are inside the pasta rather then outside in the sauce.

Begin the first step of this recipe well ahead of time because the sweetbreads must be soaked for several hours in frequent changes of water before the filaments can be removed and the sweetbreads readied for chopping.

> *1 pound fresh sweetbreads*
> *½ cup white wine vinegar*
> *1¼ cups olive oil*
> *1 cup plus 2 tablespoons chopped yellow onions*
> *2 teaspoons finely minced garlic*
> *¼ pound sweet Italian sausage,* peeled and chopped*
> *2 teaspoons salt*
> *½ teaspoon freshly ground black pepper*
> *⅛ teaspoon freshly grated or ground nutmeg*
> *⅓ cup cooked spinach, thoroughly drained, and finely chopped*
> *5 cups flour*
> *4 eggs, lightly beaten*
> *2¼ cups freshly grated Parmesan cheese*
> *2 pounds fresh mushrooms, thinly sliced*
> *2 cups chopped Polpa al Pomodoro (Tomato Pulp), page 4*
> *2 tablespoons chopped fresh parsley*
> *3 quarts boiling water*
> *1 tablespoon salt*
> *4 tablespoons sweet butter*

1. Wash sweetbreads in cold water, then soak in cold water for 2 hours, changing water several times. Very carefully pull off, with your

---

* Avoid Tuscan *finocchiona* and other fennel-flavored sausages.

fingers, as much of the filaments as you can without tearing the flesh. Soak them again for 2 hours, this time in several changes of cold water with 1 tablespoon of white wine vinegar per quart.

2. Remove and delicately peel off as much more of the filament as you can. Chop very fine. They are now ready for inclusion in the recipe.

3. Heat ¼ cup of the olive oil in saucepan, and add 2 tablespoons onion, 1 teaspoon garlic, the sweetbreads, sausage, ½ teaspoon salt, ¼ teaspoon black pepper, and nutmeg. Sauté, over very low heat, for 10 minutes, stirring. Drain away most of the liquid the sweetbreads have rendered. Add the spinach and cook for 3 more minutes, stirring. Remove from heat. Purée in blender. (Yields about 1½ cups.)

4. Make a mound of the flour on a large pastry board, and make a well in the middle. Place sweetbread-sausage-spinach mixture, the lightly beaten eggs, and ¼ cup Parmesan cheese in well of flour. Work into flour, kneading for at least 20 minutes, adding a little more flour if necessary. Divide dough into two or more parts and roll out each part as thinly as possible on a floured surface (according to instructions for rolling out pasta in recipe for plain Egg Pasta, page 51. Stretch dough sheets on clean towels to dry for about ½ hour.

5. While dough is drying, heat 1 cup of the remaining olive oil in a saucepan. Add the remaining cup of chopped onions and sauté, stirring, over low heat, until onions are translucent. Add the remaining teaspoon of garlic and the sliced mushrooms. Sauté, stirring, for 5 minutes, then add Tomato Pulp, parsley, and the remaining 1½ teaspoons salt and ¼ teaspoon black pepper. Cook, over moderate heat, stirring frequently, for 30 minutes. Remove from heat and keep hot. (Yields about 5 cups.)

6. Fold each sheet of dough like a rolled newspaper, and cut across dough with a sharp knife, making ribbons ¾ inch wide (unless, of course, you use a pasta machine). Shake ribbons loose and cook in boiling salted water for 3 minutes. Drain well and place in large heated bowl. Add 1 cup of Parmesan cheese and toss.

7. Add butter and 2 cups of the tomato-mushroom sauce and mix thoroughly. Serve with remaining sauce in gravy boat and with a bowl of remaining Parmesan cheese.

SERVES 6 TO 8

TAGLIOLINI FREDDI
COLD THIN EGG NOODLES
North Italy

Traditionally, this has been in Italy a summer after-theater—or after-opera—dish.

> 1 recipe Pasta all'Uovo *(Egg Pasta)*, page 51
> 3 quarts boiling water
> 1 tablespoon salt
> 1 teaspoon finely minced garlic
> ½ cup finely chopped fresh parsley
> 1 teaspoon finely chopped fresh basil *
> 1 cup olive oil
> 1 quart Salsa al Pomodoro a Crudo *(Cold Tomato Sauce)*,
>   page 6

1. When the Egg Pasta has dried, take each strip, roll up lightly like a newspaper, and cut each roll with a sharp knife into strips about ⅛ inch wide.
2. Unroll strips, and add to boiling salted water. As soon as strips rise to the top, cook for about 3 more minutes. Drain thoroughly and place on serving platter.
3. Mix garlic, 5 tablespoons parsley, basil, and olive oil, and add immediately to the pasta. Toss gently but thoroughly and let mixture cool completely (do not chill).
4. Make a well in the center of the pasta and fill it with the Cold Tomato Sauce. Garnish center of tomato sauce with 3 tablespoons chopped parsley. Mix at table, when serving.

SERVES 6 TO 8

* If dried basil is used soak it in the olive oil for at least 10 minutes.

TORTELLINI IN BRODO   *Emilia-Romagna*
TORTELLINI IN BROTH

Tortellini in Brodo is the traditional dish served during Christmas, New Year's Eve, and Twelfth Night festivities in Bologna, and, with some slight variations, in most of the regions of Emilia-Romagna. The following is the basic recipe for making and cooking tortellini. Cooking and serving them in broth, however, is only one way to present them. Tortellini *al sugo* served either with meat sauce or tomato sauce are equally delicious.

There is a popular story behind the creation of tortellini. According to a nineteenth-century poem by Giuseppe Cori (based on a passage from a seventeenth-century poem by Tassoni, entitled "La Secchia Rapita" ["The Abducted Bucket"]), Venus, Mars, and Bacchus came down to earth to defend the people of Modena, threatened by the people of Bologna who had stolen a famous bucket (which still exists), a precious symbol to the people of Modena. Venus, Mars, and Bacchus spent their first night in an inn at Castelfranco, near Modena, "giving themselves delectation for a long time." The poem says that Venus woke up after a long refreshing sleep, and not finding her companions—they had gone down to the kitchen to reinforce their strength with a zabaione made with one hundred eggs— she gave such a pull to the bell as to make the whole abode resound. The innkeeper, who was from Bologna, ran to answer the imperious call and found himself in the presence of the goddess. Inspired by her beauty, he dashed back to the kitchen and, handling between his thumb and forefinger a piece of egg pasta, "imitating the belly button of Venus," the art of making tortellini began.

This is obviously a festa dish—as well as it should be with the amount of handicraft involved. We found it ideal to make with four good-tempered people working together: one to make the dough, a sheet at a time so the dough doesn't get too dry, and three others to sit around a table, stuffing, folding, and gossiping.

> *¼ pound turkey or chicken breast*
> *¼ pound lean loin of pork*
> *¼ pound lean veal*
> *1 tablespoon sweet butter*
> *¼ pound lean prosciutto*

¼ *pound mortadella* *
8 eggs
1¼ cups freshly grated Parmesan cheese
½ *teaspoon salt*
¼ *teaspoon freshly ground black pepper*
¼ *teaspoon freshly grated or ground nutmeg*
6 cups sifted flour
1½ tablespoons olive oil
1½ tablespoons tepid water
3 quarts Brodo Classico *(Classic Broth)*, *page 35*

1. Remove the ligaments from the turkey or chicken breast. Lightly sauté the turkey or chicken, pork, and veal in the butter. Pass these meats, plus the prosciutto and mortadella, through a meat grinder very fine. Place the ground meats in a bowl together with 2 eggs, ¼ cup Parmesan cheese, the salt, black pepper, and nutmeg. Mix well into a thick paste and place in refrigerator until ready to use.

2. Make a dough with the flour, 6 eggs, olive oil, and water. Knead it well and let it rest, covered, for 15 minutes.

3. Roll dough very thin on floured surface following the directions for Egg Pasta, page 51, and cut into circles, 1½ to 2 inches in diameter. Using the back of a small spoon, place a tiny mound of filling in the center of each circle. (The trick of making tortellini is to put as much filling as possible into the dough circles which are as small as one can manipulate, so that you taste the stuffing more than the dough.)

4. Double dough over filling into half circles and pinch the edges together. Then fold the top of the half circle down over the stuffing without flattening it. Take the two "points" of the dough, fold them around your index finger, and press them together firmly. The resulting ringlets must not ooze stuffing. As soon as all the tortellini are folded, plunge into boiling Classic Broth and cook, simmering, for at least 15 minutes. Contrary to the usual practice of cooking pasta *al dente*, tortellini should be well cooked, or the dough at the folds of the "envelopes" will remain tough. Serve tortellini in the Classic Broth with a bowl of remaining Parmesan cheese.

MAKES ABOUT 180 TORTELLINI
SERVES 8 TO 10

* Mortadella sausage is available in shops specializing in Italian food.

GNOCCHI   *North Italy*
Gnocchi

Gnocchi is a very old Italian food. In the twelfth century it was certainly known although old texts refer to it indiscriminately as gnocchi or macaroni. In any case they were made only with flour and water (in some parts of Italy they are still done that way). Only the introduction into Italy of potatoes made the final differentiation. Today, in Northern Italy, Gnocchi are dumplings made with flour, potatoes, and water; sometimes with the addition of spinach, cheese, eggs, etc., or a mixture of cereals, such as farina, cornmeal, etc., and water; cooked, cooled, cut in lozenges, and baked with the addition of butter and cheese, or sauces and cheese. Macaroni of course is a variety of dry pasta used all over Italy. It is curious to notice that all dry pasta (spaghetti, linguini, *maccheroncelli,* vermicelli, etc.) in the deep South of Italy and among the Italo-Americans in the United States were called macaroni until fairly recently.

3 quarts boiling water
2 tablespoons plus 1 teaspoon salt
5 medium potatoes
2 egg yolks
1½ cups flour (more, if needed)
¼ cup plus 2 tablespoons sweet butter, melted (more, if desired)
1½ cups freshly grated Parmesan cheese

1. Cook potatoes in 3 quarts boiling water, to which you have added 1 tablespoon salt, for about 30 minutes or until tender. Drain and place in saucepan. Mash potatoes, while cooking over very low heat, to get rid of excess water.

2. Mix together the mashed potatoes, egg yolks, 1 teaspoon salt, and flour. Knead mixture well in a bowl or on a floured board into a dough. Roll by hand on a floured board into long sausagelike rolls about the shape of a thick cigar. Cut into pieces about 1 inch long. Press pieces over front of fork, rolling gently, to flute and curve them slightly.

3. Plunge Gnocchi in 3 more quarts boiling water to which you have added remaining 1 tablespoon salt. As soon as they rise to surface, remove

with slotted spoon, place on hot serving dish, and repeat operation until all Gnocchi are cooked. Add butter and ½ cup Parmesan cheese. Toss and serve with remaining Parmesan cheese in a bowl.

SERVES 6

VARIATIONS:

Gnocchi alla Bolognese: Serve Gnocchi with 2 cups of Bolognese Sauce, page 10.

Gnocchi alla Salvia: Using the same amount of butter, brown it with 1 tablespoon of fresh sage, and then toss it with Gnocchi.

Gnocchi alla Genovese: Serve Gnocchi with 1 cup of Pesto, Genoa Style, page 14.

Gnocchi alla Piemontese: Using the same amount of butter, brown it and then toss with Gnocchi. Add ¼ pound fontina cheese, sliced very thin, and place on piping hot Gnocchi. Serve with 2 cups of Tomato Sauce, page 4, separately, in a gravy boat.

Gnocchi del Buongustaio: After tossing Gnocchi with butter, slice 1 medium white truffle paper thin, and sprinkle on top just before serving. Serve with 2 cups of Meat Juice, page 8, separately, in a gravy boat.

STROZZAPRETI ALLA FIORENTINA   *Tuscany*
CHEESE AND SPINACH DUMPLINGS, FLORENCE STYLE

The literal translation of *strozzapreti* is "it strangles priests." Why this should be so, in a Catholic country, is something no one has yet explained. But the name, in various dialects, crops up for more than one dish in Italian cuisine.

> *1 pound spinach*
> *½ cup boiling salted water*
> *1¼ cups ricotta cheese*
> *4 egg yolks*
> *1½ cups freshly grated Parmesan cheese*
> *¼ teaspoon salt*
> *¼ teaspoon* Quattro Spezie *(Four Spices), page 3*
> *1 cup flour*
> *3 quarts boiling water*
> *1 tablespoon salt*
> *2 cups hot* Sugo di Carne *(Meat Juice),* page 8*
> *4 tablespoons sweet butter*

1. Remove tough parts of spinach and wash carefully. Bring spinach to a boil in salted water and drain immediately. Chop very fine and drain again thoroughly.

2. In a bowl mix together spinach, ricotta, egg yolks, ½ cup Parmesan cheese, ¼ teaspoon salt, and ¼ teaspoon of Four Spices to a very smooth paste.

3. With a regular tablespoon ladle out a piece of the mixture and roll it between floured hands into a small, bite-sized ball. Repeat until the mixture is used up, always keeping your hands floured.

4. Bring lightly salted water to a simmer, then carefully add the dumplings, one at a time, being very careful that there are not too many in the pot at any one time or they will stick together. Remove each dumpling as soon as it rises to the surface. Drain well. Place in a heated serving

---

* If you don't have Meat Juice on hand, simply serve with more butter and Parmesan cheese.

dish, cover with the hot Meat Juice,* sprinkle with ½ cup Parmesan cheese, dot with small pieces of butter, and gently toss. Serve with a bowl of remaining Parmesan cheese.

SERVES 4 TO 6

SARDENAIRA   *Liguria*
PIZZA, LIGURIA STYLE

Pizza is usually exclusively identified with Southern Italy, but in fact all along the coast, from Naples to Marseilles, variations of pizza are found. It is known as pizza in the South, *sardenaira* in Liguria, and *pissaladiere* in Nice and Marseilles. According to a poem-cookbook from the Augustan period called *Moretum*, this dish was known to the ancient Romans—although without the tomatoes, which were unknown to them.

> 1½ teaspoons powdered yeast
> ½ cup warm water
> 1½ cups flour
> 1¼ teaspoons salt
> 4 tablespoons sweet butter, softened
> 1 egg, beaten
> 6 tablespoons olive oil
> ⅓ cup finely chopped yellow onion
> 2 cups chopped Polpa al Pomodoro *(Tomato Pulp)*, page 4
> 12 anchovy fillets, puréed
> ¼ teaspoon freshly ground black pepper
> 1 teaspoon dried oregano
> ½ teaspoon finely minced garlic
> 1½ tablespoons small capers
> 20 black olives, pitted and coarsely chopped

1. Soften the yeast in the warm water.
2. Sift the flour and 1 teaspoon salt in a large bowl. Make a depression in center of flour and add the yeast-water mixture, butter, and beaten

egg. With your hands mix into a ball of dough. If dough is too thick, add a little warm water, and end mixing by kneading with hands on a floured surface, until dough is smooth and pliable. Form again into a ball, place in large, floured mixing bowl, cover with damp cloth, and let rise in warm place for 2 hours, or until double in bulk.

3. In the meantime prepare the sauce. Heat 4 tablespoons olive oil in a skillet or heavy pan. Add the onions, Tomato Pulp, puréed anchovies, ¼ teaspoon salt, black pepper, oregano, and garlic. Cook over low heat, stirring, for 5 minutes, or until anchovy purée is completely mixed in.

4. When the dough has risen, divide into two pieces.

5. Preheat oven to 400° F.

6. Oil two 8-inch pie pans with remaining 2 tablespoons olive oil. With your fists flatten the dough gently but quickly and evenly in pans to the edges, leaving a slight ridge around the edges. Spread each dough-lined pan with tomato-anchovy sauce. Dot surfaces with capers and olives. Place in preheated oven for about 25 minutes or until crust is golden and sauce bubbling.

SERVES 6 TO 8

RICE

RISOTTO

Risotto con Zafferano alla Milanese
Risotto Verde

Risotto con Punte d'Asparagi
Risotto con Funghi

Risotto con Fegatini di Pollo alla Piemontese

RISOTTO CON ZAFFERANO ALLA MILANESE

Lombardy

SAFFRON RISOTTO, MILAN STYLE

According to several sources, the use of saffron in recipes like Saffron Risotto, Milan Style, and other dishes of Lombardy grew out of the Renaissance practice, in the houses of the rich, of gilding their food, not only because so much importance was given to appearance, but also because alchemists believed that gold was good for the heart. Then, during the seventeenth-century Spanish domination of the Duchy of Milano, saffron was introduced. Its brilliant gold color suggested immediately its substitution for the much more expensive gilding. Now, of course, it is an integral part of many of the dishes of Lombardy, which is one of the few regions in Italy where it is used to any great extent. In Italy one of the only remaining uses of real gilding is the gold coating of almonds served at fiftieth wedding-anniversary celebrations.

In Italy, when a risotto is cooked to its proper degree of perfection, it is often referred to as a *"risotto all'onda." All'onda* means "like a wave." This means that the grains of rice do not stick together, but the risotto is still very moist and succulent.

We must give fair warning to the cook: This dish requires rather hard work in the sense that the risotto needs constant attention and stirring and it is not a dish that can be made ahead of time.

> ½ *cup sweet butter*
> ½ *medium yellow onion, finely chopped*
> 3 *tablespoons beef marrow (optional)*
> 1 *teaspoon freshly ground white pepper*
> 1 *cup dry white wine*
> 2½ *cups uncooked long grain rice*
> 1 *teaspoon salt*
> ¼ *teaspoon crushed saffron*
> 5 *cups (more, if needed) boiling* Brodo di Pollo *(Chicken Broth),*
> *page 36*
> 2 *cups freshly grated Parmesan cheese*

77

1. Melt 6 tablespoons butter in a large heavy pan or casserole, and add the onion, marrow (if used), and white pepper. Cook over very low heat until onion is golden and soft.

2. Add the white wine and cook over moderate heat, until wine is reduced by one-half. Add the rice and salt, and cook, stirring, for 2 to 3 minutes, or until wine is absorbed.

3. Add saffron and 1 cup of Chicken Broth. Cook until absorbed, stirring constantly. Continue to add broth, 1 cup at a time, stirring almost constantly, until rice is tender but firm. Total cooking time will take 35 to 40 minutes.

4. Mix in the remaining 2 tablespoons butter and 1 cup of Parmesan cheese. Remove from heat, and serve with a bowl of remaining Parmesan cheese.

SERVES 6 TO 8

RISOTTO VERDE   *Liguria*
GREEN RISOTTO

6 tablespoons sweet butter
1 cup finely chopped scallions, including the tender part of the green stem
½ cup chopped fresh parsley
1½ cups finely chopped raw spinach
2 cups uncooked long grain rice
4 cups boiling Brodo di Pollo (Chicken Broth), page 36
1½ teaspoons salt
½ teaspoon freshly ground white pepper
1 cup freshly grated Parmesan cheese

1. Melt 5 tablespoons butter in large heavy saucepan or casserole, and add the scallions, parsley, and spinach. Sauté over low heat for about 5 minutes, stirring occasionally.

2. Add rice and cook, stirring, until thoroughly mixed with vegetables.

3. Add 2 cups of Chicken Broth, salt, and white pepper, and cook until absorbed, stirring occasionally. Continue adding 1 cup of broth at a time, stirring almost constantly until rice is tender but firm. Remove from heat, and mix in the remaining tablespoon butter and the Parmesan cheese.

SERVES 6

RISOTTO CON PUNTE D'ASPARAGI *Emilia-Romagna*
RISOTTO WITH ASPARAGUS TIPS

2½ pounds fresh asparagus
2 quarts boiling water
1 teaspoon salt
½ cup sweet butter
½ cup chopped yellow onion
¼ teaspoon freshly ground black pepper
1 cup dry white wine
2 cups uncooked long grain rice
5 cups boiling Brodo di Pollo *(Chicken Broth)*, *page 36*
1½ cups freshly grated Parmesan cheese

1. Wash and clean asparagus, cutting off tough ends, and cook in boiling salted water for about 15 minutes, or until tender but still firm. Drain well and set aside.

2. Melt 6 tablespoons butter in a large heavy pan or casserole, and add the onion and black pepper. Sauté, over very low heat, until onion is golden and soft. Add the white wine and cook over high heat, until wine is reduced by one-half.

3. Add the rice and stir well until all the butter and wine are absorbed.

4. Add 1 cup Chicken Broth, and cook until absorbed, stirring constantly. Continue to add broth, 1 cup at a time, stirring almost constantly, until rice is tender but firm. Total cooking time will take 35 to 40 minutes.

5. About 2 minutes before the rice is done, add the asparagus tips, finish cooking, and remove from heat.

6. Add remaining 2 tablespoons butter, ½ cup Parmesan cheese, and mix well. Serve with a bowl of remaining Parmesan cheese.

SERVES 6

RISOTTO CON FUNGHI *Liguria*
Risotto with Mushrooms

½ cup sweet butter
2 medium yellow onions, finely chopped
1 teaspoon freshly ground white pepper
1 cup dry white wine
2½ cups uncooked long grain rice
1 teaspoon salt
1 ounce dry mushrooms, soaked in tepid water for 20 minutes, squeezed dry, and chopped
5 cups boiling Brodo di Pollo *(Chicken Broth)*, page 36
2 cups freshly grated Parmesan cheese

1. Melt 6 tablespoons butter in a large heavy pan or casserole, and add the onions and white pepper. Sauté over very low heat until onions are golden and soft.

2. Add the white wine and cook over moderate heat until wine is reduced by one-half.

3. Add the rice and salt, and cook, stirring, for 2 to 3 minutes or until wine is absorbed.

4. Add mushrooms and 1 cup of the Chicken Broth. Cook until absorbed, stirring constantly. Continue adding broth 1 cup at a time, stirring almost constantly, until rice is tender but firm. Total cooking time will take 35 to 40 minutes.

5. Mix in the remaining 2 tablespoons butter and 1 cup Parmesan cheese. Remove from heat and serve with a bowl of remaining Parmesan cheese.

Serves 6 to 8

RISOTTO CON FEGATINI DI POLLO   *Piedmont*
ALLA PIEMONTESE
MOLDED RISOTTO WITH CHICKEN LIVERS, PIEDMONT STYLE

¾ *cup sweet butter*
1 medium yellow onion, finely chopped
3 tablespoons beef marrow (optional)
¼ *teaspoon freshly ground white pepper*
1 cup dry white wine
2½ *cups uncooked long grain rice*
2½ *teaspoons salt*
5 cups boiling Brodo di Pollo *(Chicken Broth), page 36*
2 cups freshly grated Parmesan cheese
1 pound chicken livers, sliced
¼ *teaspoon freshly ground black pepper*
⅛ *teaspoon sage*
¾ *cup* Sugo di Carne *(Meat Juice), page 8*

1. Melt 6 tablespoons butter in a large heavy pan or casserole, and add the onion, marrow (if used), and white pepper. Sauté over very low heat until onion is golden and soft.

2. Add the dry white wine and cook, over moderate heat, until wine is reduced by one-half. Add the rice and 1 teaspoon salt, and cook, stirring, for 2 to 3 minutes, or until wine is absorbed.

3. Add 1 cup of Chicken Broth, and cook until absorbed, stirring constantly. Continue to add broth, 1 cup at a time, stirring almost constantly, until rice is tender but firm. Total cooking time will take 35 to 40 minutes.

4. Mix in 2 tablespoons butter and 1 cup Parmesan cheese. Place rice in a well-buttered 9-inch angel food cake mold and keep hot.

5. Melt remaining 4 tablespoons butter in saucepan, and the sliced chicken livers, 1½ teaspoons salt, black pepper, and sage, and sauté for 2 to 3 minutes. Remove from heat and keep hot.

6. Unmold the rice onto a heated serving platter. Place the sautéed chicken livers in the central hole and cover them with the Meat Juice. Serve with a bowl of remaining Parmesan cheese.

SERVES 8

FISH

PESCE

Cosce di Rana in Frittura con Limone

Filetti di Sogliola con Scampi e Carciofini
Sfogie in Saor
Rollatini di Filetti di Sogliola Ripieni

Coda d'Aragosta al Vermut e Crèma

Cozze alla Paesana

Scampi Stufati nel Vermut

COSCE DI RANA IN FRITTURA CON LIMONE

North Italy

FRIED FROGS' LEGS WITH LEMON

1½ teaspoons chopped fresh parsley
1 small yellow onion, thinly sliced
¼ teaspoon freshly grated or ground nutmeg
½ teaspoon salt
½ teaspoon freshly ground black pepper
1½ cups dry white wine
2 dozen fresh frogs' legs
1½ cups flour
3 eggs, lightly beaten
1½ cups olive oil
2 lemons, cut in wedges

1. Make a marinade of the parsley, onion, nutmeg, salt, black pepper, and white wine. Wash and dry the frogs' legs, and place them in the marinade for at least 1 hour.

3. Remove the legs, and dry lightly. Coat with flour, and then dip into the lightly beaten eggs.

3. Heat olive oil in large skillet and brown frogs' legs in it on all sides. Drain and serve decorated with lemon wedges.

SERVES 6

FILETTI DI SOGLIOLA CON SCAMPI E CARCIOFINI   *North Italy*

FILLETS OF SOLE WITH SHRIMPS AND ARTICHOKE HEARTS

> 1 cup olive oil
> ¼ cup lemon juice
> 1½ teaspoons salt
> ¼ teaspoon freshly ground white pepper
> 2 pounds fillets of sole, cut into 2- by 1-inch pieces
> 6 large shrimps, shelled and deveined
> ¼ cup plus 2 tablespoons sweet butter
> 1 cup chopped scallions
> ¾ teaspoon freshly ground black pepper
> ½ cup Purea al Pomodoro (Tomato Purée), page 4
> ¼ cup Carpano or other dry vermouth
> 2 9-ounce boxes frozen artichoke hearts, thawed
> ½ cup heavy cream

1. Mix together the olive oil, lemon juice, ½ teaspoon salt, and the white pepper. Add the sole and the shrimp and marinate for 1 hour, turning occasionally. Drain.

2. Butter a casserole with 1 tablespoon butter. Add the sole, shrimps, scallions, ½ teaspoon black pepper, Tomato Purée, and the vermouth. Bring to a boil and cook for 5 minutes.

3. Remove from heat, drain sole and shrimps, and keep hot.

4. Melt 4 more tablespoons butter in a saucepan. Add the artichoke hearts, 1 teaspoon salt, ¼ teaspoon remaining black pepper, and sauté for about 8 minutes. If pan juices form an unattractive black liquid, drain the artichoke hearts.

5. Bring the fish pan juices to a boil and cook until thickened. Add the heavy cream and simmer until reduced by one-third. Remove from heat and add, whipping, 1 tablespoon butter.

6. Place the artichoke hearts on a hot serving platter, cover them with the sole and shrimp, and top with the reduced sauce.

SERVES 6

SFOGIE IN SAOR   *Veneto*
MARINATED FILLET OF SOLE WITH RAISINS AND PINE NUTS

Sfogie in Saor is Venetian dialect for *Sogliole in Sapore,* which means "Savory Soles." It is a dish traditionally eaten by Venetians for the *Festa del Redentore* (Feast of the Redeemer). They go out into the lagoon at sunset on barges decorated with lights and garlands of flowers and on these boats equipped with tables and chairs, they consume this dish, drink their local wine, and sing accompanied by mandolins and guitars. This is a tradition surviving from the days of the Venetian Republic. In those days the barges of the rich were obviously more ornate, sculpted and gilded. There was the celebration of the Marriage of Venice to the Sea when the doge, from the top of the *Bucintoro,* a sumptuous boat larger than all the others and rowed by galley slaves, threw a golden wedding ring into the sea, symbolizing the marriage with the sea, from which all Venice's wealth derived.

This dish is best prepared two days in advance to allow the sole the proper time to marinate.

> 2 pounds fresh fillet of sole
> 3 teaspoons salt
> 2 teaspoons freshly ground black pepper
> 2 tablespoons flour
> 1 cup plus 1 tablespoon olive oil
> 1 cup chopped carrots
> 2 medium yellow onions, chopped
> 1 cup chopped celery hearts
> 2 bay leaves, crushed
> ¼ cup plus 1 tablespoon raisins
> ¼ cup plus 1 tablespoon pignoli (pine nuts)
> ¾ cup imported white wine vinegar *
> 1¾ cups Soave Bolla or other dry white wine

* Do not use tarragon or other herb-flavored white wine vinegar.

1. Flatten the fillets of sole very thin with a pounder between pieces of wax paper. Cut flattened fillets into strips approximately 7 to 8 inches long by 1 inch wide.

2. Mix together 1 teaspoon salt, the black pepper, and the flour, and dust sole strips lightly on both sides.

3. Heat 1 cup olive oil in extra large heavy frying pan or skillet. Add the fillet strips and cook for about 1 minute on each side over moderate heat. Take great care in turning the sole strips so they don't break. Remove fillet strips, drain on paper towels, and set aside in large, shallow bowl or rimmed platter to cool. Sole strips should form a single compact layer.

4. Add to the pan juices 1 tablespoon olive oil, 2 teaspoons salt, the carrots, onions, celery, and bay leaves. Sauté over moderate heat, stirring, for about 10 to 15 minutes or until onions are golden.

5. Remove vegetables with a slotted spoon and spread on top of the sole strips.

6. Dot vegetable-covered sole strips with raisins and pine nuts.

7. Add the white wine vinegar and dry white wine to the pan juices and, over high heat, reduce by one-half. Pour liquid over sole and let cool completely. Place in refrigerator for 48 hours before serving.

SERVES 6

ROLLATINI DI FILETTI DI SOGLIOLA RIPIENI   *Tuscany*
STUFFED AND ROLLED FILLETS OF SOLE

1 cucumber
2¼ teaspoons salt
3 sweet red peppers
¼ cup plus 1 tablespoon sweet butter
1⅛ teaspoons freshly ground black pepper
¾ pound sole (about 3 fillets)
3 tablespoons dry white wine
2 tablespoons olive oil
1 tablespoon imported white wine vinegar
½ teaspoon lemon juice
2 tablespoons finely chopped fresh parsley

1. Peel and thinly slice the cucumber. Sprinkle with ½ teaspoon salt and let stand for 1 hour in a bowl covered with a plate on which you place a weight. Drain well.

2. Spear sweet red peppers with a long fork or skewer and roast over high flame on all sides until skins are black. Peel off skins under cold running water. Slice peppers, remove and discard seeds and tough fibers, and chop fine.

3. Melt 1½ tablespoons of butter in saucepan, and sauté peppers for about 5 minutes, on low heat, stirring frequently. Season with ¼ teaspoon black pepper. Remove peppers from saucepan and mash with a fork until they are almost puréed.

4. Slightly flatten the fillets of sole and season each with ½ teaspoon salt and ¼ teaspoon black pepper. Cut each in half horizontally and vertically. Place about 1½ teaspoons pepper purée on each piece of sole toward one end, then roll each into a small cylinder. Tie each roll with heavy thread.

5. Melt 3½ tablespoons butter in frying pan or skillet and briefly sauté stuffed sole rolls, turning gently, for about 4 minutes over low heat. Add white wine and cook for about 1 more minute.

6. Remove from heat and let rolls cool completely in the pan juices. When cool, remove from pan juices and place in the refrigerator. When thoroughly cold, slice each roll into rings about ¼ inch thick.

5. Drain cucumbers and dress them with a mixture of the olive oil, white wine vinegar, lemon juice, and ⅛ teaspoon black pepper. Make a bed of the dressed cucumbers on a platter, sprinkle with the parsley, and arrange the stuffed sole rings on top.

SERVES 6

CODA D'ARAGOSTA AL VERMUT E CRÉMA   *Piedmont*
GRILLED LOBSTER TAILS WITH VERMOUTH AND CREAM SAUCE

Although the dish is placed among the recipes of Piedmont, the delicious sauce is typically Torinese. It was created by the cook of the beautiful Contessa Castiglione, one of the most famous mistresses of Napoleon III.

> ¼ cup very finely chopped yellow onion
> 2 cups dry white vermouth
> ½ cup sweet red vermouth or Marsala wine
> 2 cups heavy cream
> 4 egg yolks
> 1 teaspoon salt
> ½ teaspoon freshly ground black pepper
> ¼ teaspoon cayenne pepper
> ½ cup sweet butter, softened
> 4 ¾-pound frozen lobster tails, thawed
> 1 cup olive oil
> 2 lemons, cut in wedges

1. Heat the grill very hot.

2. Place onion, along with dry and sweet vermouths, in a saucepan. Bring to a boil and cook until the vermouths are almost completely evaporated.

3. In another pan simmer cream until it is reduced by two-thirds. When cream has partially reduced, add 2 tablespoons of it to the egg yolks and mix.

4. Combine onion-vermouth mixture, reduced cream, and egg yolk-cream mixture in top of double boiler. Season with ½ teaspoon salt, ¼ teaspoon black pepper, and cayenne pepper, and cook, over boiling water, adding the butter bit by bit, beating constantly with a wire whisk until thickened. Taste for seasoning. Remove from heat and keep hot.

5. Wash the lobster tails and split in half lengthwise. Season with remaining salt and black pepper, brush with oil, and place, shell side down, on the very hot grill. Grill for about 25 minutes, turning and brushing with oil frequently. Place lobster on heated serving platter, surrounded with lemon wedges, and serve sauce separately in gravy boat.

SERVES 4

COZZE ALLA PAESANA   *Liguria*
MUSSELS, PEASANT STYLE

In this recipe the mussels are first cooked in a dry white wine and then marinated in oil and vinegar with mixed herbs. The mussels may be served as an appetizer or as a first course. If mussels are served as a first course, a dry white wine should be served, preferably Verdicchio dei Castelli de Jesi or Soave Bolla. The same wine should be used in cooking the mussels.

> 6 *dozen evenly sized mussels in tightly closed shells, thoroughly cleaned*
> 3 *cups Verdicchio dei Castelli di Jesi, Soave Bolla, or other dry white wine*
> 2 *medium yellow onions, sliced*
> 12 *sprigs of parsley plus ¼ cup chopped fresh parsley*
> 2 *bay leaves, crushed*
> 1 *teaspoon thyme*
> ½ *teaspoon freshly ground black pepper*
> ¼ *cup olive oil*
> 2 *tablespoons imported white wine vinegar*
> 2 *tablespoons chopped capers*
> ¼ *teaspoon chopped fresh chervil*
> ¼ *teaspoon chopped fresh tarragon*
> ⅔ *cup chopped scallions*

1. Place mussels, white wine, onions, parsley sprigs, bay leaves, thyme, and black pepper in large casserole or kettle. Bring to a boil, cover, then

cook over high heat for about 2 to 3 minutes, or until mussel shells open. During cooking, shake kettle several times so that mussels change position and cook evenly.

2. Drain mussels, remove meat from shells, and place in a bowl to cool. Discard vegetables, herbs, and shells. Let cooking liquid stand for 1 or 2 minutes so that any residual sand may settle to bottom.

3. Strain top part of liquid through cheesecloth into another pot and bring to a boil. Cook over high heat until it is reduced to ½ cup. Remove from heat, let cool, then mix in olive oil, white wine vinegar, capers, chervil, tarragon, the chopped parsley, and scallions. Pour sauce over mussels and toss. Serve in a bowl with toothpicks, or in individual shells or small plates with oyster forks.

SERVES 6

SCAMPI STUFATI NEL VERMUT   *North Italy*
SHRIMPS STEAMED IN VERMOUTH

1 cup dry white vermouth
1 cup water
⅓ cup thinly sliced yellow onion
⅓ cup thinly sliced celery
⅓ cup thinly sliced carrots
3 sprigs of parsley
1 bay leaf
¼ teaspoon thyme
3 peppercorns
2 pounds fresh shrimps

1. Simmer dry white vermouth, water, onion, celery, carrots, parsley, bay leaf, thyme, and peppercorns in tightly covered enameled casserole for 15 minutes.

2. Then add the shrimps in shells and simmer, covered, for 4 to 5 minutes, shaking casserole frequently.

3. Let shrimps cool in liquid. Peel and devein.

NOTE: Shrimps Steamed in Vermouth is a basic way of preparing shrimps to be used in other recipes, such as Chicken, Marengo Style, page 104, and Cheese and Shrimp Paste Canapés, page 21. Shrimps Steamed in Vermouth may be served as an entrée accompanied by a rice or pasta dish, such as Saffron Risotto, Milan Style, page 77, or Gnocchi, page 70.

SERVES 4 TO 6

POULTRY

POLLO

Pollo Fritto con Pomodori
Petti di Pollo con Carciofi alla Toscana

Pollo in Fricassea all'Antica
Pollo in Intingolo alla Friulana
Spezzatino di Pollo alla Cacciatora
Spezzatino di Pollo all'Aceto

Pollo alla Marengo

Pollo Arrosto con Patate

Cappone Arroste con le Noci

POLLO FRITTO CON POMODORI   *Liguria*
FRIED CHICKEN WITH TOMATO SAUCE

The chicken pieces for Fried Chicken with Tomato Sauce are first marinated in a rosemary–garlic-flavored marinade. If serving as an entrée, cut a 3-pound chicken into serving pieces, and serve with heated Tomato Sauce, page 4. This dish can also be used as an appetizer for a cocktail party if 3 pounds of small drumsticks are used, rather than a whole chicken. Serve Cold Tomato Sauce, page 6, as a dip for the drumsticks.

> 1 3-pound chicken, cut into frying pieces
> 6 cups olive oil
> 6 tablespoons lemon juice plus 2 lemons, cut into wedges
> 1 tablespoon chopped fresh parsley plus 12 parsley sprigs
> 1 teaspoon finely minced garlic
> 1 teaspoon ground rosemary
> 1 bay leaf, crushed
> 3 teaspoons salt
> ½ teaspoon freshly ground white pepper
> 1 cup flour
> 2 cups unflavored breadcrumbs
> 2 cups heated Salsa al Pomodoro (Tomato Sauce), page 4
> 2 tablespoons chopped fresh basil leaves (optional)

1. Place chicken pieces in marinade of 1 cup olive oil, the lemon juice, chopped parsley, the finely minced garlic, rosemary, crushed bay leaf, 2 teaspoons salt, and the white pepper. Marinate for at least 2 hours, turning chicken pieces occasionally.

2. Remove chicken from marinade, drain well, dredge in flour, then dip into breadcrumbs. Heat remaining 5 cups olive oil until almost smoking,

97

and fry chicken in it until each piece is golden brown on all sides. Cover, reduce heat, and cook for about 20 to 30 minutes, or until tender. Remove white meat several minutes before removing dark meat, since the former cooks faster and dries out more quickly. Drain chicken pieces on paper towels or brown paper, sprinkle with remaining salt and keep hot. Arrange on heated platter, and garnish with parsley sprigs and lemon wedges. Serve with heated Tomato Sauce, sprinkle with fresh basil (optional) in separate bowl.

SERVES 4

PETTI DI POLLO CON CARCIOFI ALLA   *Tuscany*
TOSCANA
FRIED CHICKEN BREASTS WITH ARTICHOKES, TUSCANY STYLE

The strong artichoke flavor which permeates the chicken and wine sauce makes this simply prepared dish something quite out of the ordinary.

> *8 small tender artichokes, tough outer leaves and stem removed, hard tips cut off, each sliced vertically into 8 pieces, and choke hairs, if any, scraped out*
> *3 tablespoons lemon juice plus 2 lemons, cut into wedges*
> *2 cups olive oil*
> *2 teaspoons salt*
> *¼ teaspoon freshly ground black pepper*
> *6 plump breasts of chicken, boned*
> *1½ cups flour*
> *1 cup dry white wine*

1. Soak cleaned and sliced artichokes in water to cover with the lemon juice for 20 to 30 minutes. Drain and dry on paper towels. Heat olive oil in deep heavy skillet and fry artichokes for about 30 minutes, over low heat, seasoning them with 1 teaspoon salt and ⅛ teaspoon black pepper, and stirring occasionally.

2. Prepare chicken breasts by shaking them in a bag with 1½ cups flour and the remaining salt and black pepper.

3. When artichokes are done, remove from skillet, drain well on paper towels and keep hot. Add floured chicken breasts to oil in skillet, brown on all sides, then cover and cook, over low heat, for about 20 minutes, or until tender, turning occasionally.

4. Drain chicken and place on heated serving dish. Pour off all but 1 tablespoon of the pan juices. Add the white wine, and cook until half is evaporated, scraping bottom of skillet for brown particles.

5. Arrange artichokes around chicken, pour wine sauce over both, and serve with lemon wedges.

SERVES 6

POLLO IN FRICASSEA ALL'ANTICA *Emilia-Romagna*
OLD-FASHIONED CHICKEN FRICASSEE

In this old recipe from Emilia-Romagna, chicken with mushroom caps and pearl onions are simmered in white wine and chicken broth and served with a cream sauce.

1 2½- to 3-pound chicken, cut into frying pieces
¼ cup flour
1 cup sweet butter
2 tablespoons olive oil
1 cup dry white wine
½ teaspoon salt
¼ teaspoon freshly ground white pepper
¼ teaspoon freshly grated or ground nutmeg
3 quarts boiling Brodo di Pollo (Chicken Broth), page 36
Bouquet garni: 2 tablespoons chopped fresh parsley, 1 teaspoon
*   thyme, and 1 crushed bay leaf*
24 small white pearl onions, peeled
24 mushroom caps
1⅓ tablespoons lemon juice
3 egg yolks
½ cup heavy cream
2 tablespoons chopped fresh parsley

1. Dry chicken pieces thoroughly and dust with flour. Heat ½ cup butter and the oil in large heavy casserole. Add chicken pieces and sauté on all sides until golden.

2. Add white wine, salt, white pepper, nutmeg, and enough Chicken Broth to cover the chicken. Bring to a boil. Add the bouquet garni and cook, uncovered, over moderate heat for ½ hour.

3. Place pearl onions and mushroom caps in separate saucepans. Add 3 tablespoons butter to each, 1 tablespoon lemon juice to the mushrooms, and cover with Chicken Broth. Bring to a boil, cover, and cook until vegetables are tender but still firm. Drain, reserving the liquids, and set aside.

4. When chicken is done, remove bouquet garni and discard. Remove chicken and keep hot. Combine vegetable and chicken liquids and simmer for 2 to 3 minutes, skimming off fat. Then raise heat, boil, and reduce quickly to about 2 cups.

5. Beat egg yolks and heavy cream in a bowl with a wire whisk. Slowly add the reduced liquid, beating constantly. Return sauce to casserole and boil for 1 minute, stirring. Add remaining 1 teaspoon lemon juice, chicken, onions, mushrooms, and remaining 2 tablespoons butter. Stir well until chicken and vegetables are well coated with the sauce. If chicken and vegetables have become too cold, simmer them in the sauce for about 5 minutes, stirring. Sprinkle with parsley.

SERVES 4 TO 6

POLLO IN INTINGOLO ALLA FRIULANA

Friuli-Venezia-Giulia

CHICKEN RAGOUT, FRIULI STYLE

Traditionally Chicken Ragout, Friuli Style, is served with a cornmeal polenta, enriched with butter and Parmesan cheese.

5 tablespoons sweet butter
⅓ cup olive oil
1½ tablespoons chopped white onion
1 large clove of garlic, peeled
1 2½- to 3-pound chicken, cut into 8 to 10 frying pieces
1 teaspoon salt
½ teaspoon freshly ground black pepper
1½ cups Soave Bolla, or other dry white wine
1 ounce dry mushrooms, soaked in water for 20 minutes, drained, and chopped
1 cup chopped imported Italian salami
¼ pound chicken livers, chopped
2 tablespoons chopped fresh parsley
¼ cup Brodo di Pollo (Chicken Broth), page 36

1. Heat butter and olive oil in large frying pan or casserole, and sauté the onion over very low heat. Just before onion is golden, add garlic clove and sauté very briefly. Add the chicken pieces and brown slightly on all sides. Season with salt and pepper. Pour in white wine and, over moderate heat, let it reduce almost completely. Remove garlic.

2. Add the mushrooms, salami, chicken livers, and parsley. Cover and cook over low heat for about 15 minutes, or until chicken is tender, stirring frequently. If the sauce gets too thick, add the ¼ cup Chicken Broth.

SERVES 4 TO 6

SPEZZATINO DI POLLO ALLA CACCIATORA

North Italy

CHICKEN STEW, HUNTER'S STYLE

The title misrepresents this dish. The chicken is simmered in a very delicate tomato-mushroom sauce flavored with white wine, Cognac, Chicken Broth, fresh basil, and parsley.

1 3½-pound chicken, cut into frying pieces
1 tablespoon salt
1 teaspoon freshly ground black pepper
5 tablespoons sweet butter
2 tablespoons olive oil
1 medium yellow onion, finely chopped
1 pound fresh mushrooms, sliced
2 teaspoons flour
½ cup dry white wine
2 tablespoons Cognac
1 cup Brodo di Pollo *(Chicken Broth), page 36*
3 cups chopped Polpa al Pomodoro *(Tomato Pulp), page 4*
2 tablespoons chopped fresh parsley
2 tablespoons chopped fresh basil

1. Season chicken pieces with 1½ teaspoons salt and ½ teaspoon black pepper.

2. In a heavy frying pan or casserole heat 4 tablespoons butter and the olive oil. Add chicken and brown, over low heat, on all sides. Remove and set aside.

3. To the pan juices add 1 tablespoon butter, the onion, the mushrooms, 1½ teaspoons salt, and ½ teaspoon black pepper. Sauté for 5 minutes, stirring, and scraping bottom for browned particles. Add flour and cook, over very low heat, stirring constantly, for about 2 minutes.

4. Add the white wine, Cognac, Chicken Broth, and Tomato Pulp, and mix well. Bring to a boil and simmer for 8 to 10 minutes, covered.

5. Add chicken pieces, cover, and cook over very low heat for another 25 minutes, stirring occasionally. Remove chicken to a heated casserole

and keep hot. Reduce mushroom sauce to about 3½ cups, stirring frequently. Remove from heat and mix in 1 tablespoon parsley and 1 tablespoon basil. Pour sauce over the chicken and sprinkle with remaining parsley and basil.

SERVES 4 TO 6

SPEZZATINO DI POLLO ALL'ACETO *Marche-Umbria*
CHICKEN STEW WITH VINEGAR

12 large anchovy fillets, soaked in milk for 10 minutes, drained, and puréed
1 teaspoon finely minced garlic
¾ cup imported white wine vinegar
1 2½-pound young chicken, cut into small frying pieces
2 teaspoons salt
¼ cup flour
¾ cup olive oil
1 teaspoon ground rosemary
¼ teaspoon freshly ground black pepper

1. Mix the purée of anchovies and finely minced garlic into a smooth paste, then stir in vinegar.
2. Wash and dry chicken pieces, then season with salt and lightly dust with flour.
3. Heat olive oil in heavy frying pan. Add rosemary, black pepper, and chicken. Brown chicken on all sides, then reduce to moderate heat. Cover and cook, turning chicken pieces occasionally, for 20 minutes, or until tender. Check white meat toward end of cooking, since it cooks faster than the dark meat. Remove white meat about 2 to 3 minutes earlier than the dark. Keep chicken hot.
4. Pour out a little more than half of the oil and add garlic-anchovy-vinegar mixture to remaining pan juices. Stir, scraping pan bottom for browned particles, and cook over moderate heat for 10 minutes or until liquid is reduced by one-half. Add chicken pieces to sauce and cook, over very low heat, for 2 minutes, stirring. Remove chicken, arrange on hot platter, pour sauce over it, and serve covered.

SERVES 4

POLLO ALLA MARENGO   *Piedmont*
CHICKEN, MARENGO STYLE

France and Italy are still at war, at least to the extent that no treaty has been agreed upon over the invention of this unusual chicken dish, made with mushrooms, shrimps, *crostini,* and fried eggs. Our research divulges the following story, however. Long before Napoleonic times, Chicken, Marengo Style was cooked by Piedmontese peasant women for festa days. Then, so the story goes, Napoleon fought and won his historic battle against the Austrian army at Marengo, in Piedmont. Happy but exhausted after the battle, he rested under a huge plane tree which still exists on the bank of the Bormida River. He ordered his aide to prepare for him a supper less monotonous than those usually produced by the Catering Corps. A peasant woman from Marengo intervened and cooked a chicken for Napoleon in the same way that she had learned from her mother and her mother before her. Either because of the war or because of her own poverty, she didn't have one of the traditional ingredients—butter. But she made shift with olive oil, the usual mushrooms, some freshwater shrimps (crayfish), and fried eggs, and offered it to the victor. Napoleon liked it so much that he incorporated it into the French cuisine, depriving the peasant woman of any credit.

This entire dish is tremendously colorful—it is effective in appearance as well as taste. Incidentally, if the addition of fried eggs sounds strange, let me reassure you that they blend in beautifully and serve as a marvellous binding for the other ingredients. And remember, if the dish sounds too elaborate, the cooking of the chicken and the steaming of the shrimps can be done the day before, in which case the final cooking—reheating the chicken, warming the shrimps in butter and vermouth, making the *crostini,* and frying the eggs—should take only 30 minutes at the most.

The chicken—sans fried eggs, shrimps, and *crostini*—is also excellent served alone. In this case, serve the chicken in the casserole and reduce the sauce to 2 cups.

⅔ cup plus 2 tablespoons water
2 teaspoons salt
1 tablespoon lemon juice
¾ cup sweet butter
1 pound mushrooms, with stems removed
1 3-pound chicken, cut into small frying pieces
¾ teaspoon freshly ground black pepper
¾ cup olive oil
1 medium yellow onion, chopped
2 tablespoons flour
1 cup dry white wine
1½ cups chopped Polpa al Pomodoro *(Tomato Pulp)*, page 4
1 teaspoon finely minced garlic
1 cup Sugo di Carne *(Meat Juice)*, page 8
1 fresh or canned small white truffle, sliced paper thin (optional)
2 tablespoons cornstarch
2 pounds shrimps, cooked according to Scampi Stufati nel Vermut *(Shrimps Steamed in Vermouth)*, page 93
1 tablespoon minced scallions
3 tablespoons dry white vermouth
8 slices white bread, crusts removed, and slices halved
8 eggs
2 tablespoons minced fresh parsley

1. Place ⅔ cup water, ⅛ teaspoon salt, the lemon juice, and 2 tablespoons butter in a saucepan. Bring to a boil and add the mushroom caps. Cover and cook over moderate heat for 5 minutes, shaking pan frequently so that mushrooms change position and cook evenly. Drain mushrooms and set aside. Reserve liquid.

2. Preheat oven to 325° F.

3. Wash and dry chicken pieces and season with 1½ teaspoons salt and ½ teaspoon black pepper. Heat ½ cup olive oil in heavy skillet until almost smoking. Add chicken and brown on all sides over high heat. Remove chicken pieces to casserole as they are browned. Lower skillet to moderate heat and pour off all but 1 tablespoon oil. Add the onion and brown lightly for 5 to 6 minutes.

4. While onion is browning, sprinkle chicken with flour and toss and stir over very low heat for 1 to 2 minutes or until flour is slightly blond. Remove from heat.

5. Add dry white wine to skillet with browned onion, scraping bottom of skillet for coagulated sautéed juices. Stir and boil for 1 minute. Add wine and onion to chicken in casserole and bring to a boil, stirring thoroughly to mix the liquid and the flour. Add the Tomato Pulp, garlic, Meat Juice, and reserved mushroom liquor. Bring to a simmer, stirring.

6. Cover partially and place in oven. Cook for about ½ hour or until chicken is tender when pierced with a fork.

7. Remove from oven, add mushroom caps and truffles (if used), and bring to a simmer on top of stove, cooking for 2 to 3 minutes. Remove from heat. Pour contents into a strainer over a saucepan. Return chicken and vegetables to casserole.

8. Skim the fat off the liquid in the saucepan, and cook sauce over high heat to reduce it to 1½ cups. If too thin, stir in a mixture of cornstarch and 2 tablespoons water, and simmer for 2 minutes. Taste for seasoning and pour sauce back over the chicken and keep hot over moderate heat. If preparing chicken and sauce in advance, casserole can be set over moderate heat, brought to a simmer, and cooked for about 10 minutes, or until chicken is warmed through.

9. Cook the shrimps as indicated in the recipe for Shrimps Steamed in Vermouth. Peel and devein the shrimps and sauté in 2 more tablespoons butter, 1 tablespoon minced scallions, ¼ tablespoon salt, and ⅛ teaspoon black pepper. Stir in the dry white vermouth, and boil for 1 minute or until liquid is almost completely evaporated. Remove from heat and keep hot.

10. Heat the remaining ¼ cup olive oil and 4 more tablespoons butter, and sauté bread over high heat until crisp and golden on both sides. Drain on paper towels and keep hot.

11. Fry the eggs, sunny-side up, in remaining butter and lightly season with remaining ⅛ teaspoon salt and ⅛ teaspoon black pepper.

12. Arrange chicken pieces in center of large heated platter and cover with the sauce. Sprinkle with parsley and surround with an alternating fanlike arrangement of the shrimps, the fried bread, and the eggs.

SERVES 8

POLLO ARROSTO CON PATATE
ROAST CHICKEN WITH POTATOES

North Italy

The traditional Italian custom is to serve Roast Chicken with Potatoes with a salad of lettuce, tomatoes, radishes, and scallions dressed with *Salsa Vinaigrette* (Vinaigrette Sauce), page 15.

1 3-pound roasting chicken
1¾ teaspoons salt
¾ teaspoon freshly ground black pepper
1¼ teaspoons finely minced fresh sage leaves, or a little more than
  ¼ teaspoon dried sage
1¼ teaspoons finely minced fresh rosemary leaves, or a little
  more than ¼ teaspoon dried rosemary
½ pound salt pork, cut into 8 2-by-8-inch slices
4 medium potatoes, peeled and cubed
3 tablespoons sweet butter, melted
3 tablespoons olive oil

1. Rub the chicken, inside and out, with a mixture of 1½ teaspoons salt, ½ teaspoon black pepper, 1 teaspoon fresh or ¼ teaspoon dried sage, and 1 teaspoon fresh or ¼ teaspoon dried rosemary.

2. Truss chicken thoroughly, then, breast side up, lay on the pieces of salt pork from top to bottom, and tie on firmly.

3. Preheat oven to 300° F.

4. Place chicken in roasting pan or large frying pan, and surround with cubed potatoes. Mix melted butter and olive oil together, and pour over chicken and potatoes. Sprinkle potatoes with mixture of remaining ¼ teaspoon salt, ¼ teaspoon black pepper, ¼ teaspoon fresh or 1/16 teaspoon dried sage, and ¼ teaspoon fresh or 1/16 teaspoon dried rosemary.

5. Roast in preheated oven 30 to 45 minutes per pound, basting very frequently. Chicken is done when drumsticks are tender when pricked, and can be moved easily in their sockets.

6. Place chicken on hot platter, remove salt pork and trussing strings, surround with potatoes, and serve with gravy made from the pan juices, if desired.

SERVES 4

CAPPONE ARROSTE CON LE NOCI   *Lombardy*
ROAST CAPON WITH WALNUT STUFFING

Any moderately experienced cook can stuff and roast a fowl, and prepare a gravy. It is the particular stuffing of this capon that makes this dish unique and one of the finest *haute cuisine* dishes of Northern Italy. This unusual stuffing consists of walnuts, crushed Almond Macaroons, and heavy cream; it is flavored with nutmeg, juniper berries, cloves, and—surprise—Parmesan cheese. It is served with a gravy made of pan juices, white wine, and Cognac.

1 *6-pound capon, with giblets*
½ *yellow onion, sliced*
1 *carrot, sliced*
2 *ribs celery, with leaves, sliced*
4 *sprigs parsley*
1 *bay leaf, crushed*
3 *cups cold water*
1 *teaspoon salt*
½ *teaspoon freshly ground black pepper*
1½ *cups finely chopped walnuts*
¾ *cup heavy cream*
1¼ *cups crushed* Amaretti *(Almond Macaroons), page 198*
½ *cup sweet butter, softened, plus* ½ *cup sweet butter, melted*
5 *egg yolks, lightly beaten*
¼ *teaspoon freshly ground white pepper*
¼ *teaspoon freshly grated or ground nutmeg*
¼ *teaspoon freshly ground juniper berries*
⅛ *teaspoon ground cloves*
1 *cup freshly grated Parmesan cheese*
10 *ounces fat salt pork, thinly sliced*
⅓ *cup olive oil*
4 *tablespoons flour*
⅛ *teaspoon cayenne pepper*
¼ *teaspoon thyme*
½ *cup dry white wine*
2 *tablespoons Cognac*

1. Bone the breast of the capon. Remove skin from neck of capon and reserve. Reserve giblets.

2. Cover the onion, carrot, celery, parsley, and bay leaf with 3 cups cold water, and bring to a boil. Add the giblets, skinned neck, and bones from breast, and simmer until liver is tender. Remove liver and reserve. Continue to simmer remaining ingredients until gizzard is tender. Remove meat, strain stock of bones and vegetables, and reserve. Remove meat from neck and chop it together with the giblets. Set aside.

3. In the meantime rub inside of capon with ½ teaspoon salt and the black pepper.

4. In a bowl mix together the chopped walnuts, heavy cream, Almond Macaroons, the softened butter, egg yolks, white pepper, nutmeg, juniper berries, cloves, ¼ teaspoon salt, and the Parmesan cheese. Loosely stuff the capon with this mixture, then sew up tightly or skewer firmly all openings. The neck skin can be used to cover the front opening, which has been widened by the boning.

5. Preheat oven to 325° F.

6. Truss legs of chicken, fold wings to back, and cover bird with salt pork strips, tied on firmly. Grease roasting pan with oil, pour ¼ cup of the melted butter over the capon, and roast in oven 2 to 2½ hours, basting frequently. Thirty minutes before capon is cooked, remove it from pan and cut off the salt pork. Strain pan drippings, and replace back in pan with the capon. Brush the breast with the remaining ¼ cup melted butter, return to oven, and cook until tender and golden.

7. Pour off pan juices. Cover capon to keep it hot. Chill juices until fat congeals on surface, and separate fat from drippings.

8. On top of the stove heat 4 tablespoons of the capon fat, and slowly stir in the flour with a wire whisk, beating vigorously, until well blended and smooth. Slowly add 2 cups of mixed pan juices and stock. Cook and stir until gravy is smooth and boiling. Add ¼ teaspoon salt, cayenne pepper, thyme, white wine, and Cognac. Continue to cook, stirring, until alcohol has evaporated, and gravy is of desired thickness. If it becomes too thick, a little more stock may be added. Last, add the chopped giblets and neck meat, mix and serve with capon.

SERVES 6

GRAVY MAKES ABOUT 2 CUPS

VEAL

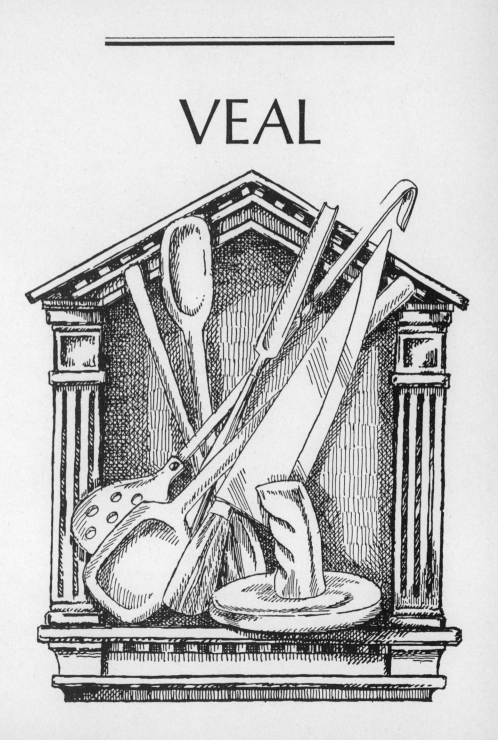

VITELLO

Osso Buco alla Milanese

Vitello Tonnato
Cima alla Genovese
Petto di Vitello Ripiene

Cotolette di Vitello alla Milanese
Cotolette di Vitello alla Milanese con Spaghetti e Tartuffi

Piccata di Vitello con Limone
Scaloppine di Vitello al Marsala
Messicani alla Milanese

OSSO BUCO ALLA MILANESE   *Lombardy*
OSSO BUCO, MILAN STYLE

Osso buco or *oss bus* (in dialect), which literally means "hollowed bone," is one of the most famous traditional dishes of Milan. It consists of veal shins, which are stewed in a tomato-wine sauce. The Milanese serve it with a small spoon for use in digging out the marrow of the bone which is considered the best part of the *osso buco*. And facetiously they call this special spoon *agente delle tasse*, "the tax collector."

Osso buco is traditionally served with *Risotto con Zaferano alla Milanese* (Saffron Risotto, Milan Style), page 77.

> *3 pounds veal shins, cut into 6 pieces about 2 inches thick*
> *½ cup flour*
> *¼ cup sweet butter*
> *1 tablespoon olive oil*
> *2 teaspoons salt*
> *½ teaspoon freshly ground black pepper*
> *1 medium yellow onion, chopped*
> *½ cup chopped carrots*
> *½ cup chopped celery*
> *1 teaspoon finely minced garlic*
> *¼ teaspoon marjoram*
> *1 teaspoon grated lemon rind*
> *1 cup dry white wine*
> *1 cup chopped* Polpa al Pomodoro *(Tomato Pulp), page 4*
> *1 cup hot* Brodo Classico *(Classic Broth), page 35*
> *½ teaspoon grated orange rind*
> *½ cup finely chopped parsley*

1. Buy veal shins that are well covered with meat. Ask your butcher to saw the bones into 6 pieces, approximately 2 inches thick.
2. Roll shin pieces in flour. Heat 3 tablespoons butter and the oil

in a heavy skillet or casserole and brown the shin pieces on all sides. Sprinkle them with salt and black pepper.

3. Add the onion, carrots, celery, ½ teaspoon garlic, the marjoram, and ½ teaspoon lemon rind. Cook over very low heat for about 10 minutes, or until vegetables are soft.

4. Add the white wine and cook until almost completely evaporated.

5. Add the Tomato Pulp and ½ cup hot Classic Broth. Cover and cook over low heat for 1½ hours, or until tender. If sauce in which the shin pieces are cooking evaporates too quickly add small amounts of hot broth from time to time.

6. When shin meat is tender mix in the remaining ½ teaspoon garlic, the remaining ½ teaspoon lemon rind, the ½ teaspoon orange rind, and the remaining tablespoon of butter. Stir and cook for 2 more minutes. Sprinkle with parsley and serve very hot.

SERVES 6

VARIATIONS:

Osso Buco in Gremolata: Omit carrots, celery, and tomatoes. This is another very traditional dish of Lombardy.

Osso Buco Laureato: Add 1 crushed bay leaf to the sautéed vegetables and ½ cup of brandy to the sauce at the end of cooking. The recipe *Osso Buco Laureato* translates as "Graduated *Osso Buco*," and refers to the bay leaf, i.e., laurel, which was used in ancient times to make the circular coronet to crown champions and, later, poets.

VITELLO TONNATO   *North Italy*
COLD VEAL WITH TUNA

This dish originated in France but became very popular in Italy, and now is an integral part of Northern Italian cuisine, especially because of the excellence of Italian tuna and the superb veal which is found in Northern Italy.

4 anchovy fillets
2 medium carrots
2 pounds boned leg of veal, fat and tendons removed, rolled and
 tied into a cylinder
1 medium yellow onion
2 large ribs of celery
2 tablespoons chopped lemon rind
1 cup dry white wine
¼ cup lemon juice
1 cup olive oil
2 cups cold water
1 teaspoon salt
1 7-ounce can imported Italian tuna fish, packed in olive oil
2 cups Salsa Maionese *(Mayonnaise)*, page 12
2 lemons, thinly sliced, each slice halved
Sprigs of parsley
2 tablespoons small capers

1. Slice julienne, 2 anchovies and 1 carrot, and with them lard the veal.

2. Slice thin the remaining carrot, onion, and celery, and place together with the veal in a large heavy pot or Dutch oven. Add the lemon rind, white wine, lemon juice, olive oil, cold water, and salt. Cover and cook over low heat for 1 to 1½ hours, or until veal is tender.

3. When done, remove the veal from the pan and set aside. Strain broth into smaller pan, place the veal back into it, and let it cool completely. When veal has cooled in the liquid, remove and dry. Over moderate heat reduce liquid by half, and reserve.

4. In a blender, or with mortar and pestle, purée together the tuna and the 2 remaining anchovies. Then add the Mayonnaise and mix thoroughly. If sauce is too thick, dilute with some of the reserved sauce.

5. Serve veal very cold, sliced very thin, topped with tuna sauce. Decorate with lemon slices, sprigs of parsley, and the remaining reserved sauce dotted with capers.

SERVES 6

CIMA ALLA GENOVESE   *Liguria*
COLD STUFFED VEAL, GENOA STYLE

This dish is one of the great specialties of Genoa. Since it is a rather expensive and elaborate recipe to prepare and since it is served cold and therefore can be made well ahead of time, it is worthwhile to make it for a fairly large group of people. It can be an excellent addition to the usual ham and turkey so often served at many American buffets.

¼ pound fresh sweetbreads
¼ cup white wine vinegar
2 pounds breast of veal
1½ pounds lean leg of veal, ground
¼ pound lean prosciutto, ground
3 slices white bread, dipped in milk, squeezed dry, and mashed
½ cup freshly grated Parmesan cheese
2 cups shelled, fresh small green peas
½ cup shelled pistachio nuts
1 teaspoon marjoram
4 eggs, lightly beaten
1 tablespoon salt
1 teaspoon freshly ground black pepper
¼ teaspoon freshly grated or ground nutmeg
1 medium yellow onion, sliced
1 medium carrot, sliced
1 bay leaf, crushed
2 peppercorns

1. Wash the sweetbreads in cold water, then soak in cold water for 2 hours, changing water several times. Very carefully pull off with your fingers as much of the filaments as you can without tearing the flesh. Soak them again for 2 hours, this time in several changes of cold water with 1 tablespoon of white wine vinegar per quart.

2. Remove and delicately peel off as much more filaments as you can and cube. They are now ready for inclusion in the recipe.

3. Have your butcher flatten the breast of veal until it is about ½ inch thick. Fold the meat in two and sew it up on two sides so that you have a bag in which to place the stuffing.

4. In a large bowl mix together the cubed sweetbreads, ground veal, prosciutto, bread, Parmesan cheese, green peas, pistachio nuts, marjoram, eggs, 2 teaspoons salt, black pepper, and nutmeg. With this stuffing fill the prepared breast of veal, then sew up the opening carefully.

5. Place the stuffed veal in a large kettle. Add the onion, carrot, bay leaf, and peppercorns. Cover with cold water, add the remaining salt, and bring slowly to a boil. Cook over moderate heat for 2 hours, then drain and place it on a board. Cover with wax paper or plastic wrap and put a heavy weight on it to compress the meat and the stuffing. Cool in refrigerator, weight and all. Before serving remove weight, wax paper, and thread and cut into thin slices.

SERVES 12

PETTO DI VITELLO RIPIENE
STUFFED BREAST OF VEAL

Marche-Umbria

2 pounds boned veal breast, cut and pounded into a 17- by 10-
    by ½-inch rectangle, or veal scallopini, pounded thin and sewn
    together into a rectangle
½ pound lean pork, ground
¼ pound ground plus ¼ pound julienne-sliced sweet prosciutto
    or ham
¼ pound ground plus ¼ pound julienne-sliced mortadella sausage
3 slices white bread, crusts removed, dipped in milk, and
    squeezed dry
½ teaspoon finely minced garlic
2 tablespoons chopped fresh parsley
¼ teaspoon freshly grated or ground nutmeg
2 eggs, lightly beaten
¼ cup sweet butter
½ cup dry red wine
1 cup milk or Brodo di Pollo (Chicken Broth), page 36

1. Trim off the rough edges of the veal breast or scallopini rectangle, until the rectangle is roughly 14 by 10 by ½ inches. Ground the veal trimmings.

2. Mix together the ground pork, prosciutto or ham, mortadella, soaked bread, garlic, parsley, nutmeg, ground veal, and lightly beaten eggs.

3. Make a layer of the mixture on half of the rectangle crosswise, or across the width of the mixture, leaving a margin of about ½ inch around the spread. Top this with a layer of the julienne-sliced prosciutto and mortadella, then with another layer of the mixture. Repeat operation until ingredients are used up. Fold veal over into an envelope and sew all three sides closely together into a pouch. Tie meat with string into a sausage shape.

4. Melt butter in heavy casserole, place veal in it, and brown well on all sides over moderate heat. Add the red wine and reduce completely. Add milk or Chicken Broth.

5. Lower flame and cook for about 1 hour, covered, basting frequently.

6. Remove from heat, untie veal, and place sliced on heated serving platter.

7. Reduce pan juices until thickened, if necessary using a bit of arrowroot diluted first in water. Pour juices over the sliced meat.

NOTE: As a *contorno* (accompaniment) and a decoration for this dish *finocchi alla Parmagiana* (fennel with Parmesan) is often served, or, if fennel is unobtainable, *sedani alla gratino* (celery au gratin). They should rim the platter of meat.

SERVES 6

COTOLETTE DI VITELLO ALLA MILANESE   *Lombardy*
VEAL CHOPS, MILAN STYLE

Contrary to general opinion, Veal Chops, Milan Style, is "mother" and not "daughter" of the Austrian Wiener schnitzel. In the State Archives in Vienna there is a document written by Marechal Radetzky regarding the political-military situation in Lombardy, at that time under Hapsburg domination. In a marginal note there is a description of a "marvelous way the Milanese people have of cooking veal chops, dipped in eggs, breaded, and fried slowly in butter." When Radetzky returned to Vienna, the Emperor Franz Joseph asked him to dictate to the Imperial chef the Milanese recipe for cooking veal chops.

6 large veal chops, flattened
2 cups milk
1 cup clarified butter
¼ cup flour
1 teaspoon salt
½ teaspoon freshly ground black pepper
¼ teaspoon freshly grated or ground nutmeg
6 eggs, beaten
2 cups unflavored breadcrumbs
¾ cup freshly grated Parmesan cheese
¾ cup dry white wine
2 lemons, cut into wedges

1. Buy milk-fed veal, between 5 and 12 weeks old. The flesh of the chops should be firm and very pale pink in color.

2. Soak the flattened veal chops in the milk for ½ hour, turning occasionally if milk doesn't cover. Remove and dry thoroughly with paper towels.

3. Brush the chops on both sides with 2 tablespoons clarified butter. Sift together the flour, salt, black pepper, and nutmeg. Dip each chop into this mixture, then dip them into the beaten eggs, and then into a mixture of the breadcrumbs and Parmesan cheese. Repeat dipping of each chop into eggs and then again into breadcrumbs and Parmesan cheese mixture. This repetition of the dipping makes a thicker crust which is less liable to flake off during the cooking, but do not *over* coat the chops.

4. Heat the remaining clarified butter in a large, heavy skillet or frying pan. Add chops and reduce heat to very low. Cook for about 15 minutes, turning chops occasionally but very carefully, trying not to break their crusts. Very low heat is necessary so that the butter does not burn.

5. Remove chops to a heated serving platter. Add the white wine to pan juices, scrape bottom for brown particles, and cook, stirring, until liquid is reduced to about ½ cup and slightly thickened. Pour over chops and serve garnished with lemon wedges.

SERVES 6

NOTE: These veal chops, without the wine and any pan juices poured over them, are also very good cold and they are as popular in picnic baskets in North Italy as fried chicken is in America.

COTOLETTE DI VITELLO ALLA MILANESE   *Lombardy*
CON SPAGHETTI E TARTUFFI
VEAL CHOPS, MILAN STYLE, WITH SPAGHETTI
AND TRUFFLE SAUCE

¼ *cup plus 2 tablespoons sweet butter*
½ *cup julienne-sliced mushrooms*
½ *cup julienne-sliced lean ham*
¼ *cup julienne-sliced black truffles*
¼ *teaspoon salt*
¼ *teaspoon freshly ground black pepper*
¼ *teaspoon nutmeg*
2 *tablespoons* Sugo di Carne *(Meat Juice), page 8, or concentrated* Brodo di Manzo *(Beef Broth), page 36*
½ *pound spaghetti, broken into 2-inch pieces, cooked, and drained*
1 *recipe* Cotolette di Vitello alla Milanese *(Veal Chops, Milan Style), page 118*

1. Melt 4 tablespoons butter in a small saucepan. Add the mushrooms and sauté, over low heat, for 10 minutes, stirring frequently. Add the ham, truffles, salt, black pepper, and nutmeg, and sauté for 2 to 3 minutes over very low heat, stirring constantly. Mix in the Meat Juice or concentrated Beef Broth. Remove from heat and keep hot.

2. Place the spaghetti back into the kettle where it has been cooked. Add the remaining butter and toss. Place the spaghetti in the middle of a heated platter, pour Truffle Sauce over it, and surround with Veal Chops, Milan Style.

SERVES 6

PICCATA DI VITELLO CON LIMONE   *North Italy*
VEAL SCALLOPS WITH LEMON

⅔ cup flour
2 teaspoons salt
½ teaspoon freshly ground black pepper
1½ pounds leg of veal, cut into 6 scallops, pounded
    1/16 inch thin
½ cup sweet butter
¼ cup lemon juice
¼ cup finely chopped fresh parsley

1. Mix together flour, salt, and black pepper.
2. Dip veal scallops in seasoned flour.
3. Melt and heat 6 tablespoons butter until it foams. Add veal scallops and cook, on very low heat, turning frequently, until brown and tender. Remove scallops and keep hot.
4. Add lemon juice, parsley, and 2 tablespoons butter to pan juices. Stir well and pour over hot scallops.

SERVES 6

SCALOPPINE DI VITELLO AL MARSALA   *North Italy*
VEAL SCALLOPS WITH MARSALA SAUCE

1½ pounds leg of veal, cut into 6 scallops, pounded 1/16 inch
    thin
½ teaspoon salt
¼ teaspoon freshly ground black pepper
2 tablespoons flour
¼ cup sweet butter
¾ cup dry Marsala wine
3 tablespoons Brodo di Pollo (Chicken Broth), page 36
1 large lemon, cut into 6 wedges
12 sprigs of parsley

1. Dip scallops lightly in a mixture of the salt, black pepper, and flour.

2. In a large heavy frying pan, heat the butter until it foams.

3. Add the veal scallops, reduce heat, and brown thoroughly on both sides, taking great care the butter doesn't burn. Since the scallops are so thin, this should be a very short process.

4. Add the Marsala to the scallops and cook for 1 more minute on moderate heat, turning frequently. Remove veal to serving dish and keep hot.

5. Add the Chicken Broth to pan, scraping bottom and sides to remove brown particles. Cook for 1 more minute, strain pan juices, and pour over meat.

6. Decorate rim of serving dish with lemon wedges and parsley sprigs.

SERVES 6

MESSICANI ALLA MILANESE — *Lombardy*
STUFFED VEAL ROLLS, MILAN STYLE

The use of garlic and lemon rind in the stuffing is a sure indication that this dish is typical of the cuisine of Lombardy. Why these veal rolls are called *messicani* (Mexicans) is something we have been unable to discover. They are skewered along with bacon slices and served with a wine sauce.

12 veal scallops, pounded almost paper thin and each measuring about 4½ to 5 inches long and 3 inches wide

¼ cup plus 2 tablespoons sweet butter

¼ pound pork loin, ground

7 ounces prosciutto fat, ground

½ teaspoon finely minced garlic

1 slice white bread, dipped in milk, squeezed dry, and mashed

1 cup freshly grated Parmesan cheese

1 teaspoon grated lemon rind

½ teaspoon freshly ground black pepper

¼ teaspoon freshly grated or ground nutmeg

2 eggs, lightly beaten

¼ cup flour, seasoned with salt and freshly ground black pepper

½ pounds Canadian bacon, sliced, and cut into 2½- by 1-inch rectangles

1 cup dry white wine, Soave Bolla or other

1 cup Brodo Classico *(Classic Broth), page 35*

1 teaspoon arrowroot, dissolved in 1 teaspoon water, if needed for thickening sauce

1. Buy milk-fed veal, between 5 and 12 weeks old. The flesh should be firm and very pale pink in color. If scallops are not reasonably even, trim to size and grind the trimmings for use in stuffing mixture.

2. Melt 2 tablespoons butter in frying pan, and sauté the ground pork for about 5 minutes.

3. In a bowl mix together, to a pasty consistency, the ground. veal trimmings (if any), pork, prosciutto fat, garlic, bread, Parmesan cheese, lemon rind, black pepper, nutmeg, and eggs. Press mixture against sides of bowl to make it firm.

4. Place 2 heaping tablespoons of the above mixture on each slice of veal. Roll up each slice and dust with seasoned flour.

5. Skewer a piece of bacon at each end with meat or wooden skewers, then add a *messicano* to the skewers (piercing it at the overlapping fold, in order to keep it closed). Add another piece of bacon, another *messicano,* and finish with a third piece of bacon. Repeat this process on individual skewers until you have six servings of 2 *messicani* and 3 bacon slices each.

6. Melt remaining butter in two large heavy frying pans. Add the *messicani* and cook, over very low heat, turning occasionally, until browned on both sides.

7. Add the white wine and Classic Broth, and cook, over moderate heat, for 15 to 20 minutes, turning *messicani* occasionally.

8. Remove *messicani* to hot platter. Scrape bottoms of pans for browned particles, and strain liquid through dampened cheesecloth into a saucepan. If sauce is too thin, stir in the arrowroot-water mixture and simmer for 2 minutes. Pour sauce over *messicani*.

SERVES 6

BEEF, LAMB, AND PORK

MANZO, AGNELLO, E MAIALE

Bistecca alla Fiorentina

Agnello Arrosto alla Toscana
Agnello Brasato in Crosta

Costolettine d'Agnello al Momento

Prosciutto Brasato alla Marsala con Funghi

Arista di Maiale alla Toscana
Lombo di Maiale in Umido

Maiale Ubriaco
Lombatine di Maiales con Salsa di Prugne

BISTECCA ALLA FIORENTINA *Tuscany*
BEEFSTEAK, FLORENCE STYLE

Bistecca alla Fiorentina traditionally is served with *Fagioli all'Uccelletto* (Beans with Garlic), page 152. It makes a surprisingly good combination and is an excellent variation from the usual baked potatoes which accompany steaks in America.

2 2-inch-thick porterhouse steaks *
1 cup olive oil
1½ teaspoons salt
1½ teaspoons freshly ground black pepper
2 lemons, cut in wedges

1. Place steak in large deep dish with olive oil, salt, and black pepper. Let steak marinate for 1 hour, turning occasionally.
2. Grill steaks over a charcoal fire about 8 minutes on each side. Do not overcook. Remove from grill, brush on both sides with oil of the marinade, and serve with lemon wedges.

SERVES 4

* When you buy your porterhouse steaks it would be advisable to have your butcher cut off the "tail" and grind it for other uses, since this part of the steak, when grilled, is too tough.

AGNELLO ARROSTO ALLA TOSCANA   *Tuscany*
BAKED LEG OF LAMB, TUSCANY STYLE

1 4-pound leg of young lamb
8 bay leaves, cut into small strips
5 cloves of garlic, sliced
1 tablespoon salt
1 teaspoon freshly ground black pepper
3 tablespoons sweet butter, melted
3 tablespoons olive oil
½ cup dry white wine

1. Preheat oven to 375° F.
2. Lard the lamb with the bay leaves and garlic slices. Rub it with salt and pepper. Place lamb on a rack in a roasting pan.
3. Mix together the melted butter and the oil and pour the mixture over the lamb. Roast in oven for 1 hour, or until meat is tender, basting frequently with pan juices.
4. Remove from oven and keep hot. Pour off all fat from roasting pan. Add the white wine, scrape bottom for brown particles, and cook, on top of the stove, stirring, for a few seconds.
5. Pour it over lamb and serve.

SERVES 6

AGNELLO BRASATO IN CROSTA   *North Italy*
BRAISED LEG OF BABY LAMB BAKED IN CRUST

3 cups sifted all-purpose flour
1 teaspoon salt
⅛ teaspoon sugar
½ cup plus 2 tablespoons sweet butter
2 tablespoons vegetable shortening

2 eggs, each lightly beaten separately
⅓ cup plus 1 teaspoon cold water
5½ tablespoons olive oil
1 6-pound leg of milk-fed baby lamb, boned, rolled, and tied
¼ pound fresh mushrooms, finely chopped
1 tablespoon minced scallions
⅛ teaspoon freshly ground black pepper
1¼ pounds sweet Italian sausages, skinned and mashed
10 ounces lean prosciutto or ham, finely chopped
1 teaspoon fines herbes: chopped parsley, chervil, tarragon, and chives
5 tablespoons dry Marsala wine
5 or 6 parsley sprigs

1. Place sifted flour, a heaping ¾ teaspoon salt, the sugar, 4 tablespoons butter, and vegetable shortening together in a large bowl. Rub the ingredients together rapidly with your fingers until the fats are broken down in pieces the size of small peas.

2. Add 1 lightly beaten egg and the cold water and blend in quickly with your hands, quickly forming the dough into a mass. If any of the flour mixture remains unincorporated, sprinkle it very lightly with droplets of cold water and add to the main dough mass. Press into a ball. Dough should just hold together; it should be malleable, but not damp and sticky.

3. Lightly flour a pastry board, place the dough on it, and with the heel of your hand rapidly press the pastry outward down on the board and away from you in firm, quick smears. This process will accomplish the final thorough blending of the flour and fat.

4. Gather the dough again into a mass and knead it briefly into a round ball. Sprinkly ball lightly with flour, wrap it in wax paper, and chill in freezer for about 1 hour, or in refrigerator for at least 2 hours or overnight. Dough should be firm but not congealed.

5. Melt 4 tablespoons butter in large frying pan along with 4 tablespoons olive oil. Add lamb and brown, over low heat, on all sides. Lower flame even further and cook lamb for about 30 more minutes, turning occasionally. Drain lamb and let it cool.

6. Squeeze the chopped mushrooms in the corner of a dish towel to get rid of as much excess liquid as possible.

7. Melt 1 tablespoon butter with ½ tablespoon olive oil in a saucepan,

and lightly sauté the mushrooms and scallions. Season with ⅛ teaspoon salt and ⅛ teaspoon black pepper.

8. Mix together the mashed sausages, chopped prosciutto or ham, the *fines herbes,* and the mushroom–scallion mixture.

9. When dough is chilled, remove from refrigerator and roll out as quickly as possible on a lightly floured board. If the dough is too hard, beat it with the rolling pin to soften it, then knead it briefly into a flat circle. Lightly flour the top of the dough, then roll it out on the floured surface with firm, even strokes to a thickness of about ⅛ inch. If necessary to prevent sticking, lightly flour the board and top of dough from time to time. Dough should now be used immediately.

10. Preheat oven to 350° F.

11. Spread the sausage-prosciutto-mushroom-scallion mixture evenly over the dough almost to the edges.

12. Place the cooled lamb in center of the stuffing and fold dough up around the meat until edges meet and lamb is completely enclosed. Edges of dough should just barely overlap; if not, trim off excess dough, press meeting edges together firmly so that meat and stuffing are completely encased in an envelope of dough. Brush sealed edges with a mixture of 1 beaten egg and 1 teaspoon cold water.

13. Make a hole about ¼ inch in diameter in the top center of the pastry and insert into it a funnel or "chimney" made of heavy duty aluminum foil. Seal bottom of funnel into dough with strip of leftover pastry and brush with egg-water mixture. Place meat thermometer in funnel and press through stuffing to center of lamb.

14. Grease bottom of heavy baking or roasting pan with approximately 1 tablespoon butter and 1 tablespoon olive oil. Place pastry-covered lamb in it and roast in middle section of oven for about 50 minutes, or until meat thermometer reads about 140° F. and crust is crisp and golden. During the roasting period, pour 1 tablespoon of Marsala down the funnel every 10 minutes.

15. When done, remove lamb to heated serving platter. Decorate the top where the pastry has been pinched together and the hole from which the funnel and thermometer have been removed with sprigs of parsley.

16. To serve, slice vertically, as you would a piece of sausage, so that each portion shows a ring of crust, an inner ring of stuffing, and a center of pink lamb. As you slice, take care to remove the trussing strings before serving.

SERVES 6 TO 8

COSTOLETTINE D'AGNELLO AL MOMENTO *North Italy*
LAMB CHOPS WITH TOMATO SAUCE, LEMON JUICE, AND PARSLEY

2 tablespoons lemon juice
4 tablespoons chopped fresh parsley
2 cups hot Salsa al Pomodoro alla Semplice *(Easy Tomato Sauce)*,
  page 5
6 loin lamb chops, boned and flattened
½ teaspoon salt
¼ teaspoon freshly ground black pepper
½ cup olive oil

1. Add the lemon juice and the parsley to the hot Easy Tomato Sauce. Stir and keep hot.

2. Season the lamb chops with the salt and black pepper. Heat the olive oil in a large heavy skillet or frying pan until smoking. Add lamb chops to pan and briefly sauté on both sides until lightly browned. Remove from pan with slotted spoon, place on heated platter, cover with the Easy Tomato Sauce, and serve.

SERVES 6

PROSCIUTTO BRASATO ALLA MARSALA CON FUNGHI   *Emilia-Romagna*

HAM BRAISED IN MARSALA WITH MUSHROOM SAUCE

¼ pound fresh mushrooms, chopped very fine
6 tablespoons sweet butter
1½ tablespoons olive oil
1 tablespoon minced scallions
⅛ teaspoon salt
⅛ teaspoon freshly ground black pepper
½ cup sliced yellow onion
½ cup sliced carrots
1 3-pound mild-cooked ham with bone, skinned and trimmed of
   excess fat, or 2 pounds boned cooked ham
1 cup dry Marsala wine
1½ cups Brodo di Manzo *(Beef Broth)* , *page 36*
3 sprigs parsley
1 small bay leaf
Pinch of thyme
2 tablespoons confectioners' sugar
2 teaspoons arrowroot
3 tablespoons cold liquid (the mushroom liquor supplemented by
   as much Marsala or broth as necessary)

1. Squeeze the chopped mushrooms in a thin dish towel as hard as possible in order to get rid of excess liquid, but reserve liquid for later use.

2. Melt 1 tablespoon butter and ½ tablespoon olive oil in a saucepan and very lightly sauté mushrooms and scallions. Season with the salt and black pepper and set aside.

3. Preheat oven to 325° F.

4. Melt 2 tablespoons butter and 1 tablespoon olive oil in large heavy casserole; add onion and carrots and cook, over low heat, until lightly browned.

5. Place the ham in the casserole and add the Marsala, Beef Broth, parsley, bay leaf, and thyme. Bring to a simmer on top of the stove, then cover and place in oven. Bake slowly for 1¼ hours, basting every 20 minutes. When ham is tender, remove from oven and sprinkle evenly with confectioners' sugar. Raise oven temperature to 450° F. and glaze ham in it for 10 to 15 minutes. Remove from oven and keep warm.

6. With ladle and paper towels degrease the braising liquid and cook it on top of stove until it is reduced to approximately 1½ cups. Strain into a saucepan, discarding vegetables.

7. Blend the arrowroot into the mushroom liquid mixture and add to the braising liquid. Mix in the mushrooms and scallions and simmer for about 5 minutes, tasting for seasoning. Add the remaining 3 tablespoons butter bit by bit until it is thoroughly melted and blended in. Pour into a gravy boat.

8. Slice ham and serve with sauce.

SERVES 6

ARISTA DI MAIALE ALLA TOSCANA *Tuscany*
ROAST LOIN OF PORK, TUSCANY STYLE

The name *Arista,* according to legend, is derived from the comment that a Greek archimandrite (a high priest in the Greek Orthodox Church) made when he first tasted a version of this pork roast in fifteenth century Florence. He said *Aristos,* which in Greek means "the best," and it is supposedly from this comment that the name derives.

This dish is equally good served hot or cold. In Italy the pork is typically served with a bean dish, such as *Fagioli all'Uccelletto* (Beans with Garlic), page 152, or *Fagioli al Vino Rosso* (Kidney Beans Cooked in Red Wine), page 151.

> *1 4½-pound loin of pork*
> *1 tablespoon dried rosemary*
> *3 cloves garlic, sliced*
> *2 teaspoons salt*
> *¾ teaspoon freshly ground black pepper*
> *2 cups dry white wine or dry vermouth*

1. Preheat oven to 450° F.

2. Trim the excess fat off the pork, leaving enough for pan juices. Lard the meat with the rosemary and garlic slices. Dust with salt and pepper. Tie roast securely, place in roasting pan, and roast at 450° F. for 45 minutes.

3. Pour off fat, if necessary, and reduce oven heat to 350° F. Pour the white wine or vermouth over the pork. Roast for about 2¼ hours longer, basting frequently. The inside temperature of the roast should be about 185° F.

4. After removing roast from oven, let it sit for 10 to 15 minutes. Remove string before serving.

SERVES 6

LOMBO DI MAIALE IN UMIDO   *Emilia-Romagna*
PORK LOIN IN EGG–LEMON SAUCE

1 1½-pound loin of pork, boned, rolled, and tied
1 teaspoon salt
4 tablespoons butter
½ cup chopped celery
½ teaspoon finely minced garlic
¼ teaspoon freshly ground black pepper
¼ teaspoon freshly grated or ground nutmeg
4 cups hot Brodo Classico (Classic Broth), page 35
3 egg yolks, beaten
¼ cup lemon juice

1. Rub the loin of pork with the salt.

2. Melt the butter in a Dutch oven or large heavy casserole. Add the pork loin, celery, and garlic, and, over low heat, brown meat on all sides.

3. Season with black pepper and nutmeg. Stir and add 2 cups of Classic Broth. Cover, bring to a boil, then cook over moderate heat for 1½ to 2 hours. Remove meat from pan and keep hot.

4. Strain pan juices and put in a double boiler. In the meantime slowly

add about ½ cup of the Classic Broth to the egg yolks, stirring. Mix in the lemon juice. Add egg-lemon-broth mixture to the pan juices, beating constantly. Add remaining Classic Broth, mix, and let the sauce thicken.

5. Slice the meat and pour the Egg–Lemon Sauce on top.

SERVES 4 TO 6

MAIALE UBRIACO   *Tuscany*
BRAISED PORK CHOPS WITH WINE SAUCE

The literal translation of the title of this recipe is "Drunken Pig."

6 ½-pound pork chops
2 teaspoons salt
½ teaspoon freshly ground black pepper
½ cup olive oil
1½ teaspoons finely minced garlic
3 tablespoons chopped fresh parsley
1 cup dry Chianti or other dry red wine

1. Trim the fat off the pork chops, and season with the salt and black pepper.

2. Heat the olive oil in a skillet until almost smoking, and add the pork chops and cook, over high heat, until browned on both sides. Cover and cook, over low heat, for about 30 minutes, turning occasionally.

3. Remove chops from skillet and keep hot. Pour off all but 2 tablespoons oil. Add the garlic and parsley, and sauté, over very low heat, until garlic is lightly browned. Add the red wine and, over high heat, reduce liquid to about ½ cup. Pour wine sauce over chops and serve.

SERVES 6

LOMBATINE DI MAIALE CON SALSA DI PRUGNE *Lombardy*

Loin Pork Chops with Prune Sauce

6 tablespoons butter
1 medium yellow onion, chopped
3 ounces lean prosciutto, chopped
½ cup white wine vinegar
30 medium prunes, soaked in tepid water for 20 minutes, and pitted
¾ cup boiling water
1 bay leaf, crushed
½ cup Sugo di Carne *(Meat Juice)*, page 8, or Brodo di Manzo *(Beef Broth)*, page 36
6 ½-pound loin pork chops
2 teaspoons salt
½ teaspoon freshly ground black pepper
3 tablespoons olive oil
1½ cups dry white wine

1. Melt the butter in a saucepan, and add the onion and the prosciutto, and sauté, over very low heat, until onion is golden.
2. Add the white wine vinegar and cook, over moderate heat, until half is evaporated.
3. Add the prunes, water, bay leaf, and Meat Juice or Beef Broth. Cover and cook, over low heat, for 30 minutes, or until prunes are very soft. Remove from heat and drain, reserving liquid.
4. Purée the prune mixture and dilute, stirring well, with reserved liquid. Keep hot.
5. Trim the fat off the chops, and season with the salt and pepper.
6. Heat the olive oil in a skillet, until almost smoking, and add the pork chops. Cook, over high heat, until browned on both sides. Pour off all the fat and add the white wine. Cover, and cook over low heat, for 30 minutes. Remove from heat and serve covered with the prune sauce.

Serves 6

VARIETY
MEATS
AND SAUSAGE

FRATTAGLIE E SALSICCIE

Fegato alla Milanese
Fegato alla Veneziana

Fegatini di Pollo alla Salvia

Zampone con Lenticchie

Bollito Misto

FEGATO ALLA MILANESE
CALF'S LIVER, MILAN STYLE

Lombardy

---

1 teaspoon salt
½ teaspoon freshly ground black pepper
¼ cup plus 2 tablespoons flour
2 pounds calf's liver, cut into 12 ½-inch-thick slices
6 eggs, lightly beaten
4 cups unseasoned breadcrumbs
½ cup sweet butter
1½ cups dry red wine
2 lemons, cut in wedges

1. Sift together the salt, black pepper, and flour. Dip each slice of liver into this mixture, coating thoroughly, then dip into beaten eggs, and next into the breadcrumbs.

2. Melt butter in two large heavy frying pans. When butter begins to foam, add liver slices and reduce heat to very low. Cook for about 2½ minutes on each side.

3. Remove liver to heated platter. Add red wine to pan juices, and scrape bottom of pan for brown particles. Cook, over moderate heat, until wine is reduced by half. Pour wine sauce over liver, and serve garnished with lemon wedges.

SERVES 6

FEGATO ALLA VENEZIANA   *Veneto*
CALF'S LIVER WITH ONIONS, VENICE STYLE

2 tablespoons olive oil
2 tablespoons sweet butter
3 cups thinly sliced yellow onions
1½ pounds calf's liver, cut into 6 thin slices
1½ teaspoons salt
½ teaspoon freshly ground black pepper
2 lemons, cut in wedges

1. Heat olive oil and butter in a skillet. Add the sliced onions and cook, over very low heat, for 15 to 20 minutes, or until golden and soft, stirring occasionally.

2. Add the liver, salt, and black pepper, and cook over high heat 3 minutes, stirring constantly.

3. Remove from heat and serve with lemon wedges.

SERVES 6

FEGATINI DI POLLO ALLA SALVIA   *Marche-Umbria*
CHICKEN LIVERS WITH SAGE

¾ cup sweet butter
¼ cup olive oil
8 slices white bread, crusts removed, and slices halved
1 tablespoon crushed sage
1 pound chicken livers
1¼ teaspoons salt
¼ teaspoon freshly ground black pepper
3½ ounces lean prosciutto, cut into thin strips
½ cup dry white wine

1. Heat 4 tablespoons butter and the olive oil in skillet, and sauté bread slices until golden on both sides. Drain bread on paper towels and keep hot.

2. Melt 6 tablespoons butter in a skillet, and add the sage and chicken livers. Season with the salt and black pepper. Sauté the chicken livers for about 2 minutes over high heat, stirring; then add the prosciutto. Lower the heat, and sauté for 1 more minute, stirring.

3. Remove the chicken livers and prosciutto from skillet, and keep hot. Mix the white wine into the pan juices, scraping bottom of skillet for browned particles. Cook over medium heat for 1 minute. Mix in the remaining 2 tablespoons butter, and pour the sauce over the livers and prosciutto. Surround with fried bread slices.

SERVES 4

ZAMPONE CON LENTICCHIE   *Emilia-Romagna*
ZAMPONE WITH LENTILS

This dish is traditional for New Year's dinner, served after midnight of New Year's Eve. According to popular belief, lentils, because their shapes vaguely resemble coins, represent money. Therefore, the more lentils you eat for New Year's dinner, the more money you'll make during the year to come.

Zampone and *cotechino* are very similar large sausages from the region of Emilia-Romagna, the former a specialty of Modena and the latter of Cremona. In America they are obtainable in many Italian stores or can be ordered from such places as Manganaro's in New York City.

> 1 2-*pound* zampone *or* cotechino *sausage*
> 2 *medium yellow onions, quartered, plus 1 medium yellow onion, chopped*
> 4 *ribs celery, plus* ½ *cup chopped celery*
> 1½ *cups lentils*
> 3 *cups water*
> 2 *teaspoons salt*
> 2 *tablespoons olive oil*
> 2 *ounces lean salt pork, chopped*
> 1 *cup chopped* Polpa al Pomodoro *(Tomato Pulp), page 4*
> ¼ *teaspoon freshly ground black pepper*
> 2½ *cups* Salsa al Marsala *(Marsala Sauce), page 10*

1. Place *zampone* or *cotechino* in a kettle, cover with cold water, and let stand for 2 hours.

2. Remove *zampone* or *cotechino* from water, drain, prick it all over with a fork, and wrap it in cheesecloth. Sew up carefully and then tie all around with string. Place it in a kettle and cover with cold water. Bring to a boil. Reduce the heat, add 1 quartered onion and 2 ribs of celery, and cook, over moderate heat, for 3 hours. Remove from heat and keep hot in its water.

3. Wash the lentils, cover with water, and bring to a boil. Remove from heat and let soak 1 hour. Drain. Add the remaining quartered

onion, the remaining 2 ribs of celery, the 3 cups of water, and the salt. Bring to a boil, reduce heat, and simmer for 1 hour.

4. Remove onion and celery, and drain lentils. Reserve water in which the lentils have been cooked.

5. Heat olive oil in a saucepan, and add the salt pork, chopped onion, ½ cup chopped celery, and cook, over very low heat, until onions are golden.

6. Add the lentils, Tomato Pulp, 2 tablespoons of the reserved lentil water, and black pepper. Stir and cook over low heat for 10 to 15 minutes or until lentils have absorbed all the liquid. Remove from heat and keep hot.

7. Remove *zampone* or *cotechino* from kettle, snip off cheesecloth, drain and slice thinly. Place *zampone* or *cotechino* slices in the middle of a heated platter, and surround with lentils. Pour Marsala Sauce on *zampone* or *cotechino*.

SERVES 6

BOLLITO MISTO *North Italy*
MIXED BOILED MEATS

This great classic dish is one found nowadays in Northern Italy only in some of the most elegant, old-fashioned restaurants and in very few private houses or *palazzi*. It obviously has very little in common with the dishes served as *Bollito Misto* in most Italian restaurants or trattorias. Also, those Americans who turn up their noses at the thought of boiled meats will be completely converted by this *bollito* if it is done properly and served with the proper accompaniments.

If you are really going to assay this classic Mixed Boiled Meats, you absolutely must have the real Italian *cotechino* or *zampone* and the authentic, imported *Mostarda di Cremona*. This *mostarda* is a combination of assorted candied fruits, such as figs, apricots, pears, cherries, in clear syrup flavored with hot mustard. It is a sweet, spicy relish suggested for boiled or roasted meats and fowl, and it is available in shops specializing in Italian food. We haven't indicated these ingredients as optional, and you may have to order them by mail. The flavor of the fruits of the *mostarda,* with their deceptively sweet first taste and burning hot aftertaste, is the final fillip to make this dish.

1 *2-pound* cotechino *or* zampone *Italian sausages*
1 *medium yellow onion, quartered, plus 1 medium yellow onion,*
   chopped, plus 1 medium yellow onion, larded with 5 cloves
2 *ribs celery*
2 *tablespoons sweet butter*
½ *teaspoon finely minced garlic*
2½ *ounces chicken livers, chopped*
3 *eggs, lightly beaten*
8 *slices white bread, crusts removed, soaked in 1 cup milk,*
   squeezed dry, and mashed
10 *ounces lean prosciutto*
3 *tablespoons chopped fresh parsley plus 12 parsley sprigs*
2 *cups freshly grated Parmesan cheese*
¼ *teaspoon freshly ground black pepper*
⅛ *teaspoon freshly grated or ground nutmeg*
1 *2- to 2½-pound capon or chicken, completely boned*
½ *pound lean salt pork*
1 *2-pound eye round of beef, cut into large chunks*
1 *2-pound shank of veal, cut into large chunks*
2 *pounds calf's head or calf's foot*
1 *tablespoon salt*
1 *quart hot* Brodo Classico *(Classic Broth), page 35, or 1 quart*
   boiling water
8 *large potatoes, cleaned and peeled*
8 *large carrots, cleaned and scraped*
2 *cups* Salsa Verde *(Green Sauce), page 13*
2 *cups heated* Salsa al Pomodoro *(Tomato Sauce), page 4*
2 *14-ounce cans* Mostarda di Cremona

1. Place the *cotechino* or *zampone* sausage in a kettle, cover with cold water, and let stand for 2 hours. Drain and prick all over with fork. Wrap in three or four layers of cheesecloth, sew up carefully, then tie all around with string. Place in kettle, cover with cold water, and bring to a boil. Reduce heat to a simmer and add 1 quartered onion and 2 ribs of celery. Cook for 1 hour. Remove from heat but keep warm in its cooking liquid.

2. Melt the butter in a saucepan. Add the chopped onion and garlic. Sauté, over very low heat, until onion and garlic are lightly browned.

3. Add chopped chicken livers, and sauté very briefly (not more than 2 to 3 minutes), stirring constantly. Remove from heat and place in medium-sized bowl.

4. Add the lightly beaten eggs, bread, prosciutto, chopped parsley, Parmesan cheese, black pepper, and nutmeg. Mix well.

5. With this mixture stuff the capon or chicken. Sew up all openings tightly. Wrap in several layers of cheesecloth, sew up the cheesecloth, and further secure with strings all around the fowl. Set aside for the time being.

6. Boil the salt pork in water to cover for 15 minutes. Drain and place in large kettle together with beef, veal shank, and calf's head or foot. Cover with cold water, bring slowly to a boil, and simmer for about 5 minutes. As scum begins to rise to surface, remove with ladle or spoon. As soon as scum ceases to accumulate add 1 medium onion larded with cloves and the salt. Continue cooking for 1¼ hours. As liquid reduces, add boiling water or, preferably, hot Classic Broth.

7. Add stuffed and wrapped fowl to other meats and continue cooking for 45 minutes.

8. Remove the veal shank and keep hot. At the same time drain *cotechino* or *zampone* and place, still wrapped, into kettle with meats and cook for 1 hour.

9. Remove beef and keep hot. Add potatoes and carrots to kettle and cook for ½ hour or until tender.

10. While meats are cooking prepare the Green Sauce and the Tomato Sauce according to recipe directions.

11. Remove rest of meats and vegetables, discarding the clove-larded onion and salt pork. If beef and veal shank have become too cool, replace in broth and reheat briefly; then strain the broth and reserve for other purposes.

Remove wrappings from fowl and *cotechino* or *zampone*. Place stuffed fowl in center of large heated platter. Slice *cotechino*. Place beef, veal, calf's head or foot, *cotechino* slices, potatoes, and carrots in alternating arrangement around the fowl. Decorate with parsley sprigs. Serve with separate bowls of the Green Sauce, Tomato Sauce, and *Mostarda di Cremona*.

SERVES 8

VEGETABLES

LEGUMI

Asparagi al Burro e Parmigiano
Asparagi allo Zabaione

Fagioli al Vino Rosso
Fagioli all'Uccelletto

Funghi Ripieni

Cipolline in Agrodolce

Pisellini Dolci al Prosciutto

Friggione

Patate al Basilico
Patate con Cipolline e Lardo
Patate al Prosciutto
Patate alla Salvia e Parmigiano
Patate alla Crèma Gratinate
Polpettone di Patate e Formaggio

Pane di Spinaci

Pomodori del Ghiottone
Pomodori Ripieni
Pomodori al Gratino

Zucchettini Fritti, No.1
Zucchettini Fritti, No. 2
Zucchine Ripiene della Nonna

ASPARAGI AL BURRO E PARMIGIANO   *North Italy*
FRESH ASPARAGUS WITH BUTTER AND PARMESAN CHEESE

3 pounds fresh young asparagus
1 quart boiling water
½ teaspoon salt
¾ cup sweet butter, melted
¾ cup freshly grated Parmesan cheese

1. Break off tough ends of the asparagus where they easily bend and break. Try to make them all the same length. Scrape off the scales below the tips, and wash asparagus carefully and thoroughly. The tough ends may be reserved for making a soup broth.

2. Preheat oven to 450° F.

3. Place asparagus in frying pan or large casserole; add about 1 inch of lightly salted boiling water but do not cover asparagus with water, and cook, partially covered, for about 10 minutes or until tender but still *al dente* (firm). Drain well.

4. Place a layer of asparagus in a pyrex baking dish. Pour melted butter and sprinkle Parmesan cheese over layer. Repeat operation on successive layers of asparagus until ingredients are used up, finishing with butter and Parmesan cheese.

5. Bake in oven, uncovered, for about 4 to 5 minutes. Serve immediately.

SERVES 6

VARIATION:

Another typical Italian way of serving this dish, as the main course of a luncheon, is to serve it topped with eggs fried "sunny-side up." In this fashion it is known as *Asparagi alla Milanese* (Asparagus, Milan Style).

149

ASPARAGI ALLO ZABAIONE   *Emilia-Romagna*
ASPARAGUS WITH ZABAIONE SAUCE

Zabaione Sauce:
   2 egg yolks
   1 tablespoon water
   1 cup dry white wine
   2 tablespoons sweet butter, softened
   ¼ cup heavy cream
   ¼ teaspoon freshly ground white pepper

3 pounds fresh young asparagus
1 quart boiling water
½ teaspoon salt

1. Combine the egg yolks, water, and white wine in top of a double boiler. Place over warm water and beat with wire whisk, increasing heat of water, and continuing to beat until mixture is thick and creamy. Do not allow to boil.

2. Beat in the softened butter. Remove from hot water and mix in the heavy cream and white pepper. Keep Zabaione Sauce hot.

3. Cut the tough ends off the asparagus. Wash carefully and cook in boiling salted water for about 10 minutes according to directions for Fresh Asparagus with Butter and Parmesan Cheese, page 149. Drain well. Arrange in a single layer on platter and pour Zabaione Sauce over them.

SERVES 6 TO 8

FAGIOLI AL VINO ROSSO   *Piedmont*
KIDNEY BEANS COOKED IN RED WINE

> 1 1-pound package kidney beans
> 2 cups Piedmontese dry red wine, such as Barbera, Barolo,
>   Barbaresco, Gattinara, or Ghemme
> 6 ounces lean salt pork
> 1 large yellow onion, larded with 2 cloves
> 1 teaspoon salt
> ½ pound bacon, coarsely chopped
> 1 tablespoon flour
> 2 tablespoons sweet butter

1. Wash the kidney beans thoroughly and drain. Place in large kettle, cover with 2 quarts water and bring to a boil, covered.

2. Remove from heat and let beans soak 1 hour. Drain, replace in kettle with 1½ quarts of fresh cold water, the red wine, the salt pork, and the onion. Bring to a boil, covered, and cook for ½ hour. Add the salt and cook for another 15 minutes. Drain. Discard salt pork and onion, set beans aside.

3. Fry bacon until it is almost, but not quite, crisp, in large heavy skillet or frying pan. Add flour, bit by bit, stirring constantly so no lumps form but sauce thickens. Mix in beans and butter, and stir until beans are thoroughly reheated. Taste for seasoning and serve.

SERVES 6

FAGIOLI ALL'UCCELLETTO   *Tuscany*
BEANS WITH GARLIC

2 cups dry marrow beans
¼ cup plus 1 tablespoon olive oil
1 teaspoon finely minced garlic
½ teaspoon crushed dried sage leaves
1½ cups chopped Polpa al Pomodoro *(Tomato Pulp), page 4*
1½ teaspoons salt
¼ teaspoon freshly ground black pepper

1. Wash the marrow beans, drain, cover with water in large kettle, and bring to a boil. Remove from heat, let stand for 1 hour, then drain.
2. Cover with fresh water, bring to a boil again, reduce heat to low, cover, and cook for 1¼ hours. Drain.
3. Heat the olive oil in a skillet, and add garlic and sage. Sauté over low heat for 3 to 4 minutes. Add the beans, Tomato Pulp, salt, and black pepper. Cover and cook over medium low heat for 10 minutes, stirring occasionally.

SERVES 4 TO 6

FUNGHI RIPIENI   *Lombardy*
STUFFED MUSHROOMS

1 dozen large fresh mushrooms, each with caps at least 2 to 3
*   inches in diameter*
½ cup sweet butter, melted
¾ teaspoon salt
½ teaspoon freshly ground black pepper
1 tablespoon olive oil
3 tablespoons minced yellow onion
3 tablespoons minced scallions
¼ cup dry Marsala wine

3 tablespoons unflavored white breadcrumbs
½ cup freshly grated imported Swiss Emmenthal cheese
¼ cup freshly grated Parmesan cheese
¼ cup minced fresh parsley
2 to 3 tablespoons heavy cream

1. Preheat oven to 375° F.

2. Remove stems from mushrooms and mince fine. Squeeze minced stems tightly in corner of a dish towel to remove excess moisture. Set aside for later use.

3. Brush the mushroom caps, inside and out, with 3 tablespoons melted butter. Place the mushroom caps, hollow sides up, in lightly buttered shallow pans. Sprinkle lightly with ¼ teaspoon salt and ¼ teaspoon black pepper.

4. Heat 2 more tablespoons melted butter with the olive oil in a saucepan, and sauté the onion in it for 3 to 4 minutes, without browning. Add the scallions and minced mushroom stems and sauté over moderately high heat for 6 to 8 minutes. Add the Marsala and cook rapidly until liquid is almost completely evaporated.

5. In a bowl mix together the breadcrumbs, ¼ cup of the grated Swiss Emmenthal cheese, the Parmesan cheese, parsley, and the remaining salt and black pepper. Then, stir in the onion-mushroom-scallion mixture.

6. Blend in the heavy cream, a spoonful at a time, until the stuffing mixture is moist but still stiff enough to hold its shape in a spoon. Correct seasoning if necessary.

7. Fill mushroom caps with the stuffing. Top each with a pinch of the remaining ¼ cup grated Swiss Emmenthal cheese and the remaining 3 tablespoons melted butter.

8. Bake the stuffed caps in the top third of the oven for 15 to 20 minutes, or until the caps are tender and the stuffing is lightly browned on top.

SERVES 6

CIPOLLINE IN AGRODOLCE *North Italy*
SWEET AND SOUR PEARL ONIONS

This is a marvelous variation from the usual creamed onions so often and traditionally served with American turkey dinners at Thanksgiving and Christmas.

> *1½ pounds small white pearl onions*
> *3 tablespoons sweet butter*
> *¾ teaspoon salt*
> *¾ teaspoon freshly ground black pepper*
> *2½ tablespoons sugar*
> *¾ cup red wine vinegar*
> *¾ teaspoon flour*
> *¾ cup* Brodo di Manzo *(Beef Broth), page 36*

1. Peel the pearl onions, soak in ice water for 5 minutes, and drain.
2. Melt the butter in a large skillet, add the pearl onions in a single layer, and sprinkle with salt, pepper, and sugar. Add the red wine vinegar. Cover skillet and cook for 5 minutes over high heat. Lower heat and cook for 20 more minutes, or until onions are tender. Do not stir.
3. Remove the pearl onions to serving dish and keep hot. Add flour to pan juices, blend well, and add the Beef Broth. Cook 2 more minutes and pour gravy over the cooked pearl onions.

SERVES 6

PISELLINI DOLCI AL PROSCIUTTO *Tuscany*
PEAS WITH PROSCIUTTO

Ancient Romans used to feed their horses with unshelled peas. In Italy peas came into their own in the seventeenth century after they had become a gourmet dish in France. To eat peas in the month of May was a privilege reserved for the nobility. With the change of fashion they had become terribly expensive.

¼ cup plus 2 tablespoons sweet butter
2 tablespoons finely chopped small pearl white onions
6 cups shelled, fresh small green peas
1 teaspoon salt
½ teaspoon freshly ground black pepper
¼ teaspoon sugar
3 tablespoons Brodo Classico *(Classic Broth), page 35*
6 ounces prosciutto, shredded

1. Melt butter in saucepan. Add onions and sauté until golden and soft.

2. Add the shelled peas, salt, black pepper, sugar, and Classic Broth, and cook over moderate heat for about 10 minutes or until peas are tender.

3. Add the prosciutto, and cook briskly for 2 more minutes, stirring constantly.

SERVES 6

FRIGGIONE   *Emilia-Romagna*
PEPPER, TOMATO, AND ONION STEW

This dish, the translation of which is "Big Fry," is really one of the most *campagnolo* (from *campagna,* "countryside") and cheap dishes of the Emilia-Romagna region. It is very good though, and it has become chic to serve it at elegant dinner parties in Italy together with expensive meats and other delicacies.

In Southern Italy, this dish, with the addition of vinegar, is called *peperona:a.* In Emilia-Romagna farmhouses, zucchini, in season, are often substituted for peppers. To make this vegetable dish a main course, skinned sausages are cut into thin slices and are added along with the chopped tomatoes.

> *2 pounds green and red peppers*
> *2 pounds tomatoes*
> *1 teaspoon salt*
> *2 tablespoons sweet butter*
> *¼ cup olive oil*
> *1 pound small white pearl onions, peeled and thinly sliced*
> *¼ teaspoon freshly ground black pepper*

1. Wash green and red peppers, cut off stems, remove seeds and fibers, and slice them coarsely.

2. Skin the tomatoes by dipping them briefly in boiling water, peeling, and then cutting in half. Remove water and seeds, then sprinkle insides lightly with ½ teaspoon salt, and place upside down in colander for ½ hour to let excess water drain out. Chop coarsely.

3. In a large heavy skillet heat the butter and olive oil. Add the green and red peppers and pearl onions, and cook, stirring, until onions are soft and translucent. Add the tomatoes, cover, reduce the heat, and cook for about 10 more minutes, adding the remaining salt and black pepper. Raise heat and cook, stirring, until almost all of the liquid has evaporated. Serve hot or cold, as preferred.

SERVES 6

PATATE AL BASILICO   *Liguria*
POTATOES WITH FRESH BASIL

6 medium Idaho potatoes
3 quarts boiling salted water
5 tablespoons sweet butter
2 to 3 tablespoons chopped fresh basil
Salt to taste

1. Clean and peel potatoes and cut into wedges. Cook in 3 quarts boiling salted water to cover until tender but still firm. Drain.
2. Melt butter in frying pan until foaming. Add potatoes and toss lightly until coated with butter. Sprinkle with the fresh basil and serve.

SERVES 6

PATATE CON CIPOLLINE E LARDO   *Tuscany*
POTATOES WITH PEARL ONIONS

1 pound potatoes, peeled and cut in wedges
¼ cup plus 2 tablespoons sweet butter
2 ounces lean salt pork, cooked in boiling water for 5 minutes,
  drained and cubed
1 pound small white pearl onions, cooked in boiling salted water
  for 8 minutes and drained
1 tablespoon flour
2 cups Brodo di Pollo *(Chicken Broth), page 36*
¼ teaspoon salt
¼ teaspoon freshly ground white pepper
¼ teaspoon thyme
1 bay leaf, crushed
3 tablespoons chopped fresh parsley

1. Cover potato wedges with cold water.

2. Melt butter in skillet. Add salt pork cubes, and sauté until browned. Remove salt pork and set aside.

3. Add the onions to pan juices, and sauté until tender. Remove pearl onions from skillet and keep warm.

4. Add the flour to pan juices and stir well. Mix in Chicken Broth and bring to a boil.

5. Remove potatoes from water, dry well, and add to broth-pan juices-flour mixture. Season with salt, white pepper, thyme, and bay leaf. Cook over moderate heat until potatoes are tender and liquid is almost completely absorbed. Mix in salt pork and pearl onions. Stir and cook, over low heat, for 1 to 2 minutes. Remove from heat and sprinkle with parsley.

SERVES 6

PATATE AL PROSCIUTTO   *Marche-Umbria*
POTATOES WITH PROSCIUTTO

6 medium potatoes (about 2½ pounds)
3 quarts boiling salted water
3 tablespoons olive oil
¼ pound prosciutto or ham, chopped
1 medium yellow onion, chopped
¼ teaspoon finely minced garlic
2 cups chopped Polpa al Pomodoro *(Tomato Pulp), page 4*
1 cup Brodo di Pollo *(Chicken Broth), page 36, or canned chicken consommé*
½ teaspoon salt
¼ teaspoon freshly ground black pepper
3 tablespoons chopped fresh parsley
3 tablespoons chopped fresh basil
2 tablespoons sweet butter

1. Wash potatoes and cook in 3 quarts boiling salted water for about 25 to 30 minutes or until *al dente*. Drain, peel, slice, and set aside.

2. Heat olive oil, and add prosciutto or ham and onion. Cook, stirring, until onion is golden. Add garlic, and sauté for 1 more minute, stirring. Add Tomato Pulp, Chicken Broth, the sliced potatoes, salt, and pepper. Stir, cover, and simmer on very low heat for ½ minute.

3. Add parsley, basil, and butter. Stir gently but thoroughly, and taste for seasoning.

SERVES 6

PATATE ALLA SALVIA E PARMIGIANO *Tuscany*
POTATOES WITH SAGE AND PARMESAN CHEESE

6 large potatoes, washed, peeled, and cut into wedges
3 quarts boiling salted water
½ cup sweet butter
2 teaspoons dried sage leaves, crumbled
1 cup freshly grated Parmesan cheese
½ teaspoon freshly ground black pepper

1. Boil potatoes in 3 quarts lightly salted water for barely 5 minutes (they have to remain very firm, almost *al dente*).

2. Melt butter in large heavy skillet or frying pan, add sage, and cook, over low heat, until butter is almost brown.

3. Add potatoes, stir well until potatoes have absorbed all butter and are warmed all through.

4. Mix in Parmesan cheese and black pepper, stir gently but thoroughly, remove from heat, and serve.

SERVES 6

PATATE ALLA CRÉMA GRATINATE   *Emilia-Romagna*
Potato Casserole with Cream and Cheese

2 pounds potatoes
3 quarts boiling salted water
2 cups hot light cream (more, if needed)
1 teaspoon salt
¼ teaspoon freshly ground white pepper
¼ teaspoon freshly grated or ground nutmeg
½ cup heavy cream
¼ cup sweet butter
¼ cup unflavored breadcrumbs
¼ cup freshly grated Parmesan cheese

1. Cook potatoes in 3 quarts boiling salted water for about 10 minutes, or until the outside texture is soft. Drain, peel, and cut into ½-inch-thick slices. Place potato slices in a casserole, cover with hot light cream, and season with salt, white pepper, and nutmeg. Cook, over moderate heat, for about 20 minutes, or until potatoes are tender and cream is completely reduced. Mix in heavy cream.

2. Preheat oven to 350° F.

3. Melt 2 tablespoons butter, and lightly sauté breadcrumbs. Remove from pan and drain on paper towels. Mix sautéed breadcrumbs and Parmesan cheese and sprinkle over potatoes. Melt remaining butter and pour over potatoes. Place casserole in oven and bake for 10 to 15 minutes or until surface is golden.

Serves 4 to 6

POLPETTONE DI PATATE E FORMAGGIO   *North Italy*
POTATO AND CHEESE CASSEROLE

5 medium baking potatoes
3 quarts boiling salted water
½ cup plus 1 tablespoon sweet butter
1 tablespoon plus 1 teaspoon olive oil
¼ cup flour
⅓ cup milk
1 cup (a little more than ½ pound) cubed fontina cheese
4 eggs, beaten
½ teaspoon salt
¼ cup unflavored breadcrumbs
¼ cup freshly grated Parmesan cheeese

1. Cook potatoes in 3 quarts boiling salted water for about 50 minutes, or until tender. Drain, peel, and mash coarsely with fork. Heat ½ cup butter and 1 tablespoon olive oil in a saucepan. Make a paste of the flour and milk and add it with the cheese to the pan. Cook, over moderate heat, stirring constantly until the cheese is completely melted.

2. Add the mashed potatoes, beaten eggs, and salt. Mix thoroughly and taste for seasoning.

3. Preheat oven to 350° F.

4. Grease casserole with remaining 1 teaspoon olive oil and dust with 2 tablespoons breadcrumbs. Place potato-cheese mixture in casserole, even surface with convex part of spoon, and dust with Parmesan cheese and remaining 2 tablespoons breadcrumbs. Dot surface with remaining 1 tablespoon butter.

5. Place casserole in preheated oven for 30 minutes, or until top is golden.

SERVES 6

PANE DI SPINACI   *Lombardy*
Spinach Loaf with Cream Sauce

1½ pounds fresh spinach, or 2 10-ounce packages frozen spinach
½ cup boiling salted water
2 cups Salsa Besciamella *(Béchamel Sauce), page 3*
4 eggs, lightly beaten
½ cup Parmesan cheese
¼ teaspoon salt
1 cup heavy cream
4 tablespoons sweet butter
¼ teaspoon freshly ground white pepper

1. Preheat oven to 350° F.
2. Wash spinach, drain thoroughly, discard tough stems, and chop leaves coarsely. Cook in ½ cup of boiling salted water until barely tender. Drain thoroughly and purée.
3. Place spinach purée in heavy saucepan, and cook over very low heat, stirring constantly, for about 5 minutes or until purée is dry.
4. Mix in 1 cup of the Béchamel Sauce, and continue cooking and stirring over very low heat for about 3 more minutes.
5. Remove from heat, and add the lightly beaten eggs, Parmesan cheese, and salt. Place mixture in well-buttered mold, place mold in larger vessel of shallow water 1-inch deep, and bake for about 45 minutes in the oven, or until loaf is completely firm.
6. In the meantime mix together in a saucepan the remaining Béchamel Sauce, ½ cup heavy cream, and 2 tablespoons of butter. Bring slowly to a boil, then remove from heat and mix in remaining ½ cup heavy cream, the remaining butter, and the white pepper.
7. Unmold spinach loaf onto platter and cover with the cream sauce.

Serves 6

POMODORI DEL GHIOTTONE *Tuscany*
Tomatoes Stuffed with Eggs, Mushrooms, and Ham

Literally translated, *Pomodori del Ghiottone* means "Tomatoes of the Glutton."

2½ tablespoons olive oil
5 tablespoons sweet butter
½ teaspoon finely minced garlic
½ pound mushrooms, cleaned and chopped
1¼ teaspoons salt
½ teaspoon freshly ground black pepper
¼ pound ham, chopped
6 large ripe tomatoes
4 eggs
3 tablespoons unflavored breadcrumbs

1. Preheat oven to 350° F.
2. Heat 1 tablespoon olive oil and 2 tablespoons butter in saucepan. Add the garlic, mushrooms, ¼ teaspoon salt, and ¼ teaspoon black pepper, and cook, stirring, for no more than 10 minutes. Add ham and cook, stirring, for 2 to 3 minutes more. Remove from heat.
3. Wash and clean tomatoes. Cut in half, and squeeze gently to get rid of water and seeds. Use the handle of a spoon to remove any remaining seeds. Remove part of the pulp, season tomatoes with 1 teaspoon salt and ¼ teaspoon black pepper, and place upside down on platter for 10 minutes so that any remaining fluid will drain out.
4. Beat eggs thoroughly.
5. Grease bottom and sides of very heavy frying pan with 1 tablespoon butter. Pour in the eggs and set over moderate to low heat. Stir slowly and continually until the eggs thicken to a somewhat liquid consistency.
6. Sprinkle inside of tomato halves with 1½ tablespoons olive oil, place on greased baking dish, and bake for about 10 minutes, then remove from oven.

7. Mix the mushrooms and scrambled eggs together and stuff the tomato halves with the mixture, Sprinkle tops with 3 tablespoons breadcrumbs and dot with remaining 2 tablespoons butter. Bake for about 5 more minutes, or until tops have turned golden.

SERVES 6

POMODORI RIPIENI *Lombardy*
TOMATOES STUFFED WITH MUSHROOMS

4 large, firm, ripe tomatoes
1 ¼ teaspoons salt
½ teaspoon freshly ground black pepper
2 tablespoons olive oil
5 tablespoons butter
2 medium yellow onions, chopped
½ cup chopped celery
*1 ounce dry mushrooms, soaked in water for 20 minutes, drained
    and chopped*
¼ cup chopped fresh parsley
1 slice white bread, dipped in milk, and mashed
1 cup milk
½ cup freshly grated Parmesan cheese
1 egg yolk, lightly beaten

1. Cut tomatoes in half crosswise, remove water and seeds, and season with ¾ teaspoon salt and ¼ teaspoon black pepper, and invert on colander.
2. Heat 1 tablespoon olive oil and 1 tablespoon butter in a saucepan. Add onions and celery, and sauté over low heat until onions are golden. Add the mushrooms, parsley, bread, milk, ½ teaspoon salt, and ¼ teaspoon black pepper. Mix well, and cook, over low heat, stirring constantly, until liquid is reduced and mixture is pasty in consistency. Remove from heat and let cool.
3. Add the Parmesan cheese and egg yolk, and stir.
4. Preheat oven to 325° F.

5. Place tomatoes in skillet greased with the remaining olive oil, then stuff them with the mushroom mixture. Dot tops of tomato halves with remaining butter. Bake for 20 minutes.

SERVES 8

POMODORI AL GRATINO *Liguria*
TOMATOES AU GRATIN

6 large ripe tomatoes
1 teaspoon salt
2 tablespoons olive oil
1/4 teaspoon freshly ground black pepper
2 tablespoons finely chopped fresh parsley
2 teaspoons chopped fresh oregano
1 clove garlic, finely minced
1/2 cup freshly grated Parmesan cheese
6 tablespoons breadcrumbs
6 tablespoons sweet butter

1. Wash and hull tomatoes. Cut in half. Remove water and seeds, squeezing gently; then, if necessary, use fingers or the handle of a spoon to dig out remaining seeds.

2. Sprinkle tomato halves with salt, and place upside down in colander to get rid of even more water.

3. Preheat oven to 375° F.

4. Sprinkle tomatoes with olive oil and then with black pepper.

5. Mix together parsley, oregano, garlic, and Parmesan cheese, and stuff tomatoes with the mixture.

6. Top tomatoes with small mound of breadcrumbs (1/2 tablespoon per tomato) and dot each with 1/2 tablespoon butter

7. Place stuffed tomatoes in well-oiled or buttered baking pan. Place in preheated oven and bake for 15 minutes or until tomatoes are tender and a fork pierces them easily. Baste occasionally with pan juices. Serve immediately.

SERVES 6

NOTE: The tomatoes can be prepared and stuffed well ahead of time and baked at the last minute.

ZUCCHETTINI FRITTI, NO. 1   *North Italy*
Zucchini Julienne, Deep Fried

Although these two recipes are placed in the vegetable chapter, these traditional and typical Italian *contorni* (complements) can be served as an appetizer, like potato chips—only better.

6 medium zucchini
¾ teaspoon salt
½ cup flour
4 cups olive oil

1. Cut ends off zucchini, wash and slice into long thin strips, discarding seedy part of the vegetable.
2. Place in shallow platter, sprinkle with salt, and let stand for at least ½ hour so that excess moisture is removed. Drain.
3. Dip zucchini strips in flour, then shake them in a colander to remove excess flour.
4. Heat olive oil in deep frying pan. Add zucchini and fry until crisp.

Serves 6

ZUCCHETTINI FRITTI, NO. 2   *North Italy*
Zucchini Julienne, Dipped in Egg and Fried

6 medium zucchini
¾ teaspoon salt (more, if needed)
½ cup flour
3 eggs, beaten
4 cups olive oil

1. Cut ends off zucchini, wash and slice into long thin strips, discarding seedy center of the vegetable.

2. Place strips in shallow platter, sprinkle with salt, and let stand for at least ½ hour to remove excess water. Drain.

3. Dip zucchini strips in flour, then shake them in colander to remove excess flour.

4. Dip zucchini strips into beaten eggs.

5. Heat olive oil in deep frying pan, add zucchini, and fry until crisp. (Unless you have an extra large frying pan—in which case the oil should be increased—fry the zucchini strips in small amounts so they don't stick together.) Drain and serve, sprinkling with more salt to taste.

SERVES 6

ZUCCHINE RIPIENE DELLA NONNA   *Emilia-Romagna*
STUFFED ZUCCHINI, GRANDMOTHER'S STYLE

This dish, the literal translation of which is "Grandmother's Zucchini," although placed in the vegetables chapter, obviously would make a good luncheon or supper main course, accompanied by toasted Italian bread and a mixed green salad.

12 small to medium zucchini
1 pound ground beef
¼ pound lean prosciutto or ham, ground or very finely chopped
¼ pound mortadella sausage, ground or very finely chopped (if not obtainable, increase beef and prosciutto or ham)
1 fresh or canned white truffle, chopped (optional)
6 egg yolks, plus 4 whole eggs, beaten
2 slices white bread, crusts removed, soaked in broth, squeezed dry, and mashed with fork or hands
½ cup freshly grated Parmesan cheese
¼ teaspoon salt
¼ teaspoon freshly ground black pepper
¼ teaspoon freshly grated or ground nutmeg
1½ cups flour
1 cup olive oil
¼ cup sweet butter
4 cups Salsa al Pomodoro alla Semplice *(Easy Tomato Sauce)*, *page 5*
Water or Brodo Classico *(Classic Broth), if needed, page 35*

1. Cut ends off zucchini and wash. Cut zucchini in half crosswise; make all the same length. Scoop out inside of zucchini with apple corer, being careful to leave external part intact.
2. Mix together in a bowl the beef, prosciutto or ham, mortadella, truffle (if used), egg yolks, bread, ¼ cup Parmesan cheese, salt, black pepper, and nutmeg.
3. Dust zucchini lightly with flour and dip in beaten eggs.
4. Preheat oven to 375° F.

5. Heat olive oil, add zucchini, and fry until the egg and flour coating is golden. Remove from oil.

6. Place zucchini in well-buttered casserole, in single layer (you may have to use two casseroles). Dot with remaining 3 tablespoons butter, cover with Easy Tomato Sauce, and sprinkle with remaining ¼ cup Parmesan cheese. Bake in oven for 30 minutes, adding water or Classic Broth if it gets too dry.

SERVES 8

NOTE: A simpler way of cooking these zucchini is as follows. After having stuffed zucchini as in the main recipe, heat 8 tablespoons butter in extra large frying pan (or two regular frying pans) until butter foams. Do not dip zucchini in flour and eggs, but add to frying pan with foaming butter and sauté, turning for 10 minutes. Preheat oven to 375° F. Add 4 cups Easy Tomato Sauce and enough water or broth to cover the stuffed zucchini. Bring to a boil and simmer on top of the stove for 25 minutes or until *almost* tender. Remove zucchini to baking dish. Reduce sauce by one-half. Season with 1 teaspoon salt and pour over zucchini. Sprinkle with 4 tablespoons Parmesan cheese and bake for 2 more minutes.

VARIATION: Although not typically of the Emilia-Romagna region, an excellent variation is to use Meat Juice or beef gravy instead of Easy Tomato Sauce.

SALADS

INSALATE

Insalata di Cuori di Lattuga, Aranci, e Finocchi
Insalata di Lattuga e Noci

Insalata di Aranci e Formaggio
Insalata di Pere, Formaggio, e Noci

Insalata di Riso con Asparagi, Funghi, e Tartufi

Insalata alla Russa

Insalata di Pomodori
Insalata di Pomodori con Mozzarella e Basilico

Insalata di Fagioli con Caviale

INSALATA DI CUORI DI LATTUGA, ARANCI, E FINOCCHI
Liguria

HEARTS OF LETTUCE, ORANGE, AND FENNEL SALAD

1 large fennel, tough outer leaves and ends cut off, thinly sliced
2 medium carrots, cleaned, scraped, and thinly sliced
1 cup Salsa Vinaigrette (Vinaigrette Sauce), page 15
6 hearts of lettuce, coarsely shredded
2 seedless oranges, peeled and thinly sliced

1. Place fennel and carrot slices in a large salad bowl. Add the Vinaigrette Sauce, toss, and let marinate for ½ hour.
2. Add the lettuce hearts and toss. Top with orange slices and serve.

SERVES 6

NOTE: Hearts of Boston lettuce are recommended for this salad.

INSALATA DI LATTUGA E NOCI
North Italy

ROMAINE LETTUCE AND WALNUT SALAD

1 bunch Romaine lettuce, outer tough leaves discarded, washed, and cut into pieces
2 grapefruits, halved, peeled, and cut into sections
1½ cups shelled and coarsely chopped walnuts
1 medium red onion, peeled and thinly sliced
1 cup Salsa Vinaigrette (Vinaigrette Sauce), page 15

1. Mix together the lettuce, grapefruit sections, walnuts, and red onions.
2. Dress with Vinaigrette Sauce, toss, and serve.

SERVES 6 TO 8

173

INSALATA DI ARANCI E FORMAGGIO   *Emilia-Romagna*
ORANGE AND CHEESE SALAD

6 seedless oranges
1 medium red onion
½ pound imported Swiss gruyère cheese, sliced julienne
¾ cup Salsa Vinaigrette (Vinaigrette Sauce), page 15

1. Peel the oranges and remove white underpeel and as much of the white fibers as possible. Separate into sections, remove skin, and then cut each large section into thirds.
2. Peel onion and slice into thin rings.
3. Mix orange sections, onion rings, and cheese slices together, and toss with Vinaigrette Sauce.

SERVES 6

INSALATA DI PERE, FORMAGGIO,   *Trentino-Alto Adige*
E NOCI
PEAR, CHEESE, AND WALNUT SALAD

6 pears, peeled, cored, and thinly sliced
½ cup lemon juice (only if pears are prepared ahead of time)
½ pound French or Danish Gruyère, slivered
1 cup Salsa Vinaigrette (Vinaigrette Sauce), page 15, but if
lemon juice is used on the pears leave it out of the Vinaigrette
Sauce

If salad is prepared in advance, soak the pears in the lemon juice so that they don't turn brown. Otherwise, just mix together all ingredients and toss.

SERVES 6

INSALATA DI RISO CON ASPARAGI, FUNGHI, E TARTUFI

Piedmont

RICE SALAD WITH ASPARAGUS, MUSHROOMS, AND TRUFFLE

1 *quart* Brodo di Pollo *(Chicken Broth)*, *page 36*
2 *cups uncooked long grain rice*
1 *pound fresh asparagus, cooked until tender but firm, tough ends removed, and tips diced*
2 *cups diced celery hearts*
2 *cups thinly sliced fresh mushrooms*
1 *white truffle, sliced paper thin*
4 *hard-boiled eggs, with yolks reserved*
¼ *teaspoon salt*
¼ *teaspoon freshly ground white pepper*
¼ *teaspoon paprika*
½ *teaspoon Dijon mustard*
1 *cup olive oil*
2 *tablespoons heavy cream*
3 *tablespoons lemon juice*
1 *teaspoon dry Marsala wine*

1. Bring Chicken Broth to a boil, add rice, and cook, over moderate heat, stirring with fork occasionally, for 12 to 14 minutes, or place strainer with the rice over the empty pot in which rice has been cooking until tender but firm. Drain. Place in salad bowl. Cool and toss with a fork to separate grains. Mix in asparagus, celery hearts, mushrooms, and truffle slices.

2. In a separate bowl mash the yolks of the hard-boiled eggs, and mix in the salt, white pepper, paprika, and Dijon mustard. Add the oil, bit by bit, stirring as though you were making a mayonnaise. When all oil has been added, mix in heavy cream, lemon juice, and Marsala wine. Add this sauce to the cold rice and toss.

SERVES 6 TO 8

INSALATA ALLA RUSSA　　　　　　　*North Italy*
RUSSIAN SALAD

The translation of this salad is "Russian Salad," but it is an eminently Italian dish. This salad, which consists of assorted vegetables, pickles, and eggs, and is served with Vinaigrette Sauce, was created by the cook of a foreign diplomat living in Italy in the nineteenth century, the Baron Reuss. It was first called *Insalata alla Reuss* and then it became *Insalata alla Russa*. It appears on all cold buffets and on all *carelli degli antipasti* (hors d'oeuvres carts) in Italy.

> *4 medium potatoes, cooked for 30 minutes in boiling salted water, peeled, and diced*
>
> *2 large carrots, (about 1½ cups) scraped and cooked for 30 minutes in boiling salted water, drained, and diced*
>
> *8 cauliflower flowerets cooked for 15 minutes in boiling salted water, drained, and diced*
>
> *1½ cups* Salsa Vinaigrette *(Vinaigrette Sauce), page 15 for 10 minutes in boiling salted water, drained, and diced*
>
> *1 small zucchini, washed, stem ends cut off, cooked for 5 minutes in boiling salted water, and diced*
>
> *1 cup freshly shelled peas, cooked in boiling salted water for 10 minutes*
>
> *1 small head crisp lettuce, shredded*
>
> *1½ cups* Salsa Vinaigrette *(Vinaigrette Sauce), page 15*
>
> *1 teaspoon tarragon vinegar*
>
> *½ teaspoon dry mustard*
>
> *8 anchovy fillets, soaked in milk for 10 minutes, drained, and finely chopped*
>
> *6 hard-boiled eggs*
>
> *8* cetriolini sott'aceto *(Italian pickled gherkins)*
>
> *4 tablespoons small capers*
>
> *2 cups* Salsa Maionese *(Mayonnaise), page 12*

1. Place diced potatoes, 1¼ cups of the diced carrots, diced cauliflower, diced green beans, diced zucchini, ¾ cup of the peas, and shredded lettuce into a large porcelain, glass, or earthenware bowl.

2. Mix together Vinaigrette Sauce, tarragon vinegar, mustard, and finely chopped anchovies, and add to vegetables. Toss gently.

3. Cube 4 of the hard-boiled eggs, chop 4 of the *cetriolini sott'aceto* or sour gherkins, and add along with 2 tablespoons capers to vegetable mixture. Mix in 1 cup of the Mayonnaise and toss gently but thoroughly.

4. Place salad on platter, mold into a mound and coat with remaining 1 cup Mayonnaise.

5. Slice the remaining 2 hard-boiled eggs and 4 *cetriolini sott'aceto* or sour gherkins. Decorate the salad with the remaining diced carrots, peas, sliced eggs, sliced *cetriolini sott'aceto,* and capers.

SERVES 8

INSALATA DI POMODORI   *Liguria*
TOMATO SALAD

4 medium ripe tomatoes
1 medium green tomato
1½ teaspoon salt
½ cup olive oil
2 tablespoons lemon juice
¼ teaspoon finely minced garlic
¼ teaspoon freshly ground black pepper

1. Cut tomatoes in half and squeeze each half gently to get rid of seeds and water. If necessary, use the handle of a spoon to dig out remaining seeds. Sprinkle the interiors with salt, and invert them on a platter. Let stand for about 20 minutes, drain; then slice coarsely and place in salad bowl.

2. Mix together the oil, lemon juice, garlic, and pepper, and dress the tomatoes. Toss and let marinate for at least 10 minutes before serving.

SERVES 6

INSALATA DI POMODORI CON MOZZARELLA E BASILICO   *North Italy*

TOMATO SALAD WITH MOZZARELLA AND FRESH BASIL

We recommend this delicious and unusual, but simple, salad for a first course of a summer luncheon, or, as it is used in Italy, as an accompaniment to a course of Prosciutto and Melon, page 28.

6 large ripe tomatoes
1 teaspoon plus salt to taste
1½ pounds mozzarella cheese, as fresh as possible, with a soft,
*   milky texture*
¾ cup olive oil
Freshly ground black pepper to taste
*1 cup shredded or coarsely chopped fresh basil ***

1. Halve tomatoes. Squeeze gently to remove water and seeds, and, if necessary, use the handle of a spoon to remove excess seeds. Salt and let stand, cut side down, before cutting into wedges.
2. Cut mozzarella cheese into 1-inch cubes.
3. Place tomato wedges, mozzarrella cubes, olive oil, salt, and black pepper into salad bowl and toss.
4. Top salad with the basil leaves and toss gently at the table.

SERVES 6

* If fresh basil is unobtainable or out of season, substitute 1 tablespoon dry basil soaked in the olive oil and 2 tablespoons lemon juice. Do not use lemon juice when you use fresh basil.

INSALATA DI FAGIOLI CON CAVIALE *North Italy*
WHITE BEANS AND CAVIAR SALAD

The beans in this recipe, after you add the parsley and caviar, should turn into a beautiful dark green color.

We have made this salad in larger amounts than usually would be indicated, since every time we serve it people seem to enjoy eating double their share.

2 pounds dry white beans
2 large celery ribs
4 teaspoons salt
2 large red onions, 1 sliced very thinly in rounds and halved,
*   and 1 finely chopped*
½ cup chopped fresh parsley
3¾-ounce jar fine quality black caviar
1 cup Salsa Citronette (Citronette Sauce), page 12
2 large lemons, sliced into thin rounds and halved

1. Wash the beans thoroughly and drain. Place the beans in a deep 4- to 6-quart kettle, cover with 2 quarts of water, and bring to a boil, covered. Remove from heat and let soak for 1 hour. Drain. Place the beans back in the kettle, cover with 2 more quarts fresh water, add the celery ribs, bring to a boil, and cook for 20 minutes. Add the salt and cook for 15 more minutes. Drain, discard celery ribs, and allow beans to cool completely in refrigerator.

2. Mix the beans with the chopped red onions, the chopped parsley, and the caviar. Add the Citronette Sauce and toss thoroughly. Place in a salad bowl and decorate the rim of the bowl with alternating slices of halved lemon rounds and halved onion rounds. Make also a geometrical design of the onion halves and lemon halves in the center.

SERVES 8 TO 10

DESSERTS

DOLCI

Pesche Ripiene
Pere Ripiene
Pere Ripiene allo Zabaione
Ananasso al Cioccolato
Fragole Villa d'Azzara
Mandarini Gelati in Sorpresa
Macedonia di Frutta

Gelato di Vaniglia con Salsa di Pesche
Cassata di Pistacchio e Caffe
Cassata di Fragole e Sciampagna

Zabaione
Zabaione Ghiacciato con Panna Montata e Cialde

Marchesa al Cioccolato
Sformato Dolce Fantasia
Torta di Riso

Croccante
Amaretti

PESCHE RIPIENE
STUFFED PEACHES

Emilia-Romagna

6 ripe, unblemished peaches
2 tablespoons lemon juice
2 cups dry white wine
¾ cup granulated sugar
½ teaspoon vanilla extract
1 cup heavy cream, stiffly whipped
12 Amaretti (Almond Macaroons), page 198, crushed
1 egg yolk, lightly beaten

1. Skin peaches, cut in half, and remove stones. Scoop out part of the peach pulp, and reserve. Brush the peaches inside and out with the lemon juice.

2. Bring the white wine, sugar, and vanilla extract to a boil, stirring, in a saucepan. Drop peach halves into the boiling syrup, remove from heat, and allow peaches to cool in the syrup. Drain peaches, and reserve syrup. Bring syrup to a boil, and simmer until thickened.

3. Purée the reserved peach pulp, and mix it with the whipped cream, 10 crushed Almond Macaroons, and lightly beaten egg yolk. Fill the peach halves with this mixture, place the halves in a baking pan, and chill.

4. Serve covered with the wine syrup and sprinkled with the 2 crushed Almond Macaroons.

SERVES 6

PERE RIPIENE　　　　　　　　　　　　　　　*Piedmont*
STUFFED PEARS

> *Al contadino non far sapere quanto e' buono
> il formaggio con le pere* ("Never let the peasant
> know how good cheese and pears are together").
> —Italian Proverb

*6 medium pears
1 tablespoon lemon juice
6 tablespoons sweet butter
¾ cup Gorgonzola cheese *
½ cup crushed walnuts*

1. Peel the pears and cut them in half, leaving the stem attached to one of the halves. Scoop out the seeds and 1 tablespoon of the pulp of each of the pear halves to make room for the stuffing. Brush the pears inside and out with lemon juice to keep them from turning brown.

2. Cream the butter and cheese together, stir in ¼ cup crushed walnuts, and stuff the pears with this mixture.

3. Place the pear halves back together so that there are 6 whole pears again. The stuffing will hold them together. Sprinkle the pears with the remaining crushed walnuts, patting walnuts gently into pears so that they will adhere evenly. Chill before serving.

SERVES 6

* If possible, buy fresh Gorgonzola cheese at an Italian store. The freshness and authenticity make a real difference.

PERE RIPIENE ALLO ZABAIONE   *Lombardy*
STUFFED PEARS WITH ZABAIONE SAUCE

     4 cups dry white wine
     1½ cups granulated sugar
     1 teaspoon vanilla extract
     6 large ripe pears
     6 tablespoons lemon juice
     6 ounces fresh raspberries, cleaned, or 1 10-ounce box frozen
       raspberries, thawed and drained
     Confectioners' sugar to taste
     2 teaspoons Aurum or Grand Marnier
     2 cups chilled Zabaione *(Marsala Custard)*, *page 191*
     1 cup crushed walnuts or almonds

1. Prepare a syrup by bringing the white wine, granulated sugar, and vanilla extract to a boil, stirring until sugar is thoroughly dissolved and wine is partially evaporated.

2. Remove cores and seeds of pears. With a small spoon, and working from the large, or bottom, end of the pears, remove as much of the inside pulp as possible, leaving only a shell of pear. Carefully peel the pear shells and brush them inside and out with lemon juice.

3. Chop 1 cup of the pear pulp and mix together with 2 teaspoons lemon juice.

4. Plunge pear shells into hot syrup and turn carefully for about 2 minutes or until they are coated thoroughly. Remove pears, drain, and refrigerate until completely chilled.

5. Mix together the chopped pear pulp and raspberries, and sprinkle with remaining syrup. Sweeten further with confectioners' sugar if desired. Stir in the Aurum or Grand Marnier, and chill.

6. Stuff pear shells with raspberry mixture and place each pear upright in an individual crystal dessert bowl or champagne glass.

7. Pour chilled Zabaione Sauce over pears to coat them.

8. Decorate each pear with a spoonful or more of crushed walnuts or almonds.

SERVES 6

ANANASSO AL CIOCCOLATO   *North Italy*
GLAZED PINEAPPLE WITH CHOCOLATE SAUCE

1 fresh ripe pineapple
2 cups confectioners' sugar
½ cup dark rum
3 tablespoons Kirschwasser
3 tablespoons Aurum or Grand Marnier
1 pint vanilla ice cream
1½ cups heavy cream, whipped
2 tablespoons slivered almonds
2 cups Salsa al Cioccolato *(Chocolate Sauce), page 16*

1. Peel and core fresh pineapple, being careful to remove the "eyes." Cut into 6 slices.

2. Place pineapple slices in chafing dish, and glaze, over moderate heat, adding bit by bit confectioners' sugar, dark rum, and Kirschwasser.

3. Remove from chafing dish and place in individual, chilled dessert bowls. Pour over each slice ½ tablespoon Aurum or Grand Marnier liqueur. Top with heaping tablespoons of vanilla ice cream, then with heaping tablespoons of whipped cream. Sprinkle with slivered almonds and serve with Chocolate Sauce.

SERVES 6

FRAGOLE VILLA D'AZZARA *Emilia-Romagna*
FRESH STRAWBERRIES WITH RASPBERRY PUREE AND PISTACHIO NUTS

2 12-ounce boxes frozen raspberries
3 tablespoons granulated sugar
2 tablespoons orange juice
3 tablespoons lemon juice
2¼ quarts fresh strawberries, cleaned, hulled, and halved
¼ cup confectioners' sugar
3 tablespoons Aurum or Grand Marnier
3 tablespoons Kirschwasser
2 teaspoons unsalted, shelled, and slivered pistachio nuts

1. Drain raspberries of their liquid, then purée in a blender. Stir in the granulated sugar, and the orange and lemon juices. Refrigerate.

2. Place strawberries in bowl, and sift confectioners' sugar over each layer. Add the Aurum or Grand Marnier and Kirschwasser, and refrigerate.

3. Just before serving, pour raspberry purée over strawberries and sprinkle with slivered pistachio nuts.

SERVES 6 TO 8

MANDARINI GELATI IN SORPRESA *Veneto*
SHERBET-FILLED TANGERINES SURPRISE

12 large, ripe, unblemished tangerines
¼ cup orange juice
1 cup lemon juice
1 cup granulated sugar
1 cup water
1 1-inch piece vanilla bean, split and scraped
6 tablespoons Grand Marnier

1. Cut a ¾- to 1-inch piece from the stem ends of 6 tangerines. Scoop out all of the pulp, being careful not to tear the outer skin, and reserve. Place hollowed tangerines, each with its matching top, in refrigerator, covered with plastic or aluminum foil.

2. Grate the skins of the remaining 6 tangerines. Add the reserved pulp of the 6 scooped-out tangerines. Pass pulp through a sieve, discarding the fibers and seeds. Add the orange and lemon juices to the tangerine juice.

3. Set refrigerator or freezer for maximum coldness.

4. Combine the sugar, water, and scraped vanilla bean in a saucepan. Bring to a boil over moderate heat, and cook until lightly syrupy. Remove from heat, skim, and mix with the combined fruit juices and the grated tangerine rind. Cover and let stand for about ½ hour, then strain through cheesecloth into a bowl, and beat for 30 seconds with electric beater. Pour mixture into metal tray, place in freezer for about 1 hour, or until it is well congealed.

5. Remove from freezer, spoon into mixing bowl, and beat with electric beater for another 30 seconds. Return mixture to ice tray, and replace in freezer for another hour, or until thoroughly congealed.

6. Dampen the outside skins of the hollowed tangerines with water, then fill them with the sherbet, and return to freezer for at least ½ hour. Do not replace the tops until you are ready to serve the tangerines. Just before serving sprinkle the stuffed tangerines with the Grand Marnier and replace the tops.

SERVES 6

MACEDONIA DI FRUTTA
MACEDOINE OF FRUIT

North Italy

This dessert may be varied according to which fruits are in season. Other fruit suggestions are: fresh currants, raspberries, blueberries, plums, apricots, orange wedges, pineapple, pears (all these fruits, like the peaches, should be kept in acidulated water until the last minute).

1 pound cherries
2 quarts fresh strawberries
1 pound seedless grapes
2 medium bananas
4 medium peaches
6 tablespoons lemon juice
½ to 1 cup Kirschwasser (according to taste)
2 tablespoons confectioners' sugar (more, if needed)

1. Wash and clean cherries. Make 2 slices on each side of cherries and discard center sections with pits. Place in large serving bowl.
2. Wash, hull, and quarter strawberries. Add to same bowl.
3. Wash and cut grapes in half. Add to same bowl.
4. Peel and quarter bananas vertically, then slice horizontally, adding to bowl.
5. Peel peaches, pit them, cut into small wedges, and, immediately, immerse in lemon juice. Leave in lemon juice until just before serving the *macedonia*.
6. Stir Kirschwasser and sugar into fruit mixture. Chill fruit mixture, tossing from time to time. Chill peaches, too. Drain peaches and mix into fruit mixture. Add more Kirschwasser and sugar according to taste.

SERVES 6

GELATO DI VANIGLIA CON SALSA DI PESCHE   *North Italy*
VANILLA ICE CREAM WITH PEACH SAUCE

8 medium peaches
2 tablespoons confectioners' sugar
2 tablespoons banana liqueur
½ cup Grand Marnier
1½ pints vanilla ice cream

1. Wash and dry peaches. Do not peel. Cut into chunks, discarding pits. Place in blender and blend at moderate speed until liquefied. Remove from blender, and add confectioners' sugar, banana liqueur, and Grand Marnier. Chill.

2. Place vanilla ice cream in dessert bowls, top with peach sauce, and serve remaining peach sauce separately.

SERVES 6

CASSATA DI PISTACCHIO E CAFFE   *North Italy*
CASSATA OF PISTACHIO AND COFFEE ICE CREAMS

2 tablespoons sweet butter
4 tablespoons finely crushed Croccante *(Almond Brittle), page 197*
1 quart pistachio ice cream
1 quart coffee ice cream
3 tablespoons crème de cacao or Kahlua
1 cup heavy cream, stiffly whipped

1. Chill a ten-cup mold, then butter it evenly. Coat with 2 tablespoons finely crushed Almond Brittle. Line bottom and sides with 2 cups of the pistachio ice cream.

2. Mix the coffee ice cream with the crème de cacao or Kahlua liqueur and make a second layer.

3. Mix the remaining pistachio ice cream with the whipped cream and fill mold. Cover with wax paper and freeze at very cold temperature for at least 6 hours.

4. Remove from freezer, dip mold very briefly—3 to 4 seconds—in hot water. Discard wax paper. Run a knife around the edge, invert over chilled serving plate, and knock mold sharply to release. Coat with the remaining crushed Almond Brittle, slice, and serve immediately.

SERVES 6 TO 8

CASSATA DI FRAGOLE E SCIAMPAGNA *Emilia-Romagna*
CASSATA OF STRAWBERRIES AND CHAMPAGNE

1 quart strawberries, hulled, washed, and cubed
2 tablespoons granulated sugar
1 cup good dry champagne
1 quart strawberry sherbet
1 cup heavy cream, stiffly whipped

1. Sprinkle strawberries with sugar, pour champagne over them, and chill.
2. Chill a ten-cup mold (a bread baking pan is ideal for a mold), then coat it with a layer of strawberry sherbet. Mix together the strawberry mixture and whipped cream, and fill the mold. Cover with wax paper and freeze at very cold temperature for at least 6 hours.
3. Remove from freezer, dip mold very briefly—3 to 4 seconds—in hot water. Discard wax paper, run a knife around the edge, invert over chilled serving plate, and knock mold sharply to release. Slice and serve immediately.

SERVES 6 TO 8

ZABAIONE   *North Italy*
MARSALA CUSTARD

In Italy zabaione, in its uncooked version and with less Marsala, is reserved chiefly for children and convalescents. In fact, there are bottled versions, such as *Marsala all'Uovo* (Marsala with Egg), which traditionally are given to children for energy, particularly before they go to school in winter. We give this recipe here since cooked zabaione is popular as a desert in America, although it rarely is served as such in Italy. Also, it is an ingredient in other recipes in this book.

6 egg yolks
3 tablespoons granulated sugar
⅛ teaspoon cinnamon
1 1-inch piece of vanilla bean, split and scraped
¾ cup dry Marsala wine

1. In the top of a double boiler beat together the egg yolks, sugar, cinnamon, and scraped vanilla bean with a wire whisk or rotary beater. Beat for at least 2 to 3 minutes from the moment the water starts to simmer, or until mixture is frothy, fluffy, and pale yellow.

2. Add Marsala bit by bit, beating continually. Do not let it come to a boil.

MAKES ABOUT 1 CUP

ZABAIONE GHIACCIATO CON PANNA *Emilia-Romagna* MONTATA E CIALDE

MARSALA CUSTARD AND WHIPPED CREAM DESSERT

24 egg yolks
1½ cups granulated sugar
3 cups dry Marsala wine
¼ teaspoon cinnamon
1 large sliver lemon peel
1½ pints heavy cream
¼ cup chopped walnuts (more, if desired)

1. Beat the egg yolks and sugar in top of a double boiler with a wire whisk or rotary beater until thick.

2. Beat in the Marsala. Add the cinnamon and lemon peel.

3. Place mixture in top of double boiler over hot water and beat until hot and very thick, but do not let it boil. Remove from heat, discard lemon peel, pour into large bowl, and let it get tepid.

4. Beat heavy cream with wire whisk or electric beater until thick and stiff.

5. Mix whipped cream with Zabaione Sauce.

6. Pour Zabaione-whipped cream mixture into individual bowls. Decorate center of each bowl with a teaspoon of chopped walnuts. Refrigerate until serving time. Serve with slices of shortbread.

SERVES 12

NOTE: Do not overdecorate this dessert: the pale yellow of the zabaione and the beige of the walnuts is perfect.

MARCHESA AL CIOCCOLATO   *North Italy*
CHOCOLATE CAKE-CUM-MOUSSE

10 ounces bitter chocolate
2½ cups milk
8 egg yolks
1¾ cups granulated sugar (more, if needed)
¾ cup sifted flour
1½ cups sweet butter, whipped
8 egg whites
1 cup dry white wine
Dash of vanilla extract
1½ quarts strawberries, cleaned and hulled
6 tablespoons Kirschwasser

1. Mel. the chocolate and the milk together in top of double boiler. Blend together well, then set aside to let cool, but do not chill.

2. Place egg yolks and ¾ cup of the sugar in a bowl, and beat with a wire whisk until creamy and smooth.

3. Preheat oven to 375° F.

4. Add the chocolate mixture, the sifted flour, and the whipped butter to eggs and sugar, beating continuously until thoroughly blended.

5. Beat egg whites until quite stiff, then gently fold them into the other mixture.

6. Pour mixture into a well-buttered ten-cup mold. An Italian *scannellato*, or fluted mold, would be preferable, but a large angel food cake pan

will serve. Place mold in larger pan of water (do not, of course, submerge it) and partially cover it, leaving room for steam to escape. Bake in oven for 1¼ hours.

7. While the chocolate mixture is baking, prepare the following strawberry sauce: Mix together the white wine, the remaining 1 cup sugar, and vanilla extract, and cook, stirring, over moderate heat for about 45 minutes or until sugar is dissolved and wine partially evaporated. The proper texture of the syrup is reached when a droplet stretches between the thumb and forefinger but breaks very quickly. Remove syrup from heat and let cool.

8. Place strawberries, about ½ cup of syrup, and Kirschwasser in blender at high speed until thick. Taste, and, if necessary, add extra sugar, and blend in well. Chill.

9. Remove mold with chocolate mixture from oven and let mixture chill completely.

10. Plunge mold briefly into very hot water, invert onto chilled serving platter, and knock mold sharply to release and remove it.

11. Coat chocolate mold evenly with strawberry sauce and serve any remaining sauce in a sauce or gravy boat. If desired, vanilla ice cream may be served in the center of the mold.

SERVES 8 TO 10

SFORMATO DOLCE FANTASIA   *North Italy*
Rum-Flavored Sponge Cake Souffle

1 pint chocolate ice cream
½ pound black cherries, split and pitted
8 4- by 2- by ½-inch slices sponge cake
½ cup medium rum
1 pint vanilla ice cream
1 large banana, peeled and thinly sliced

1. Chill a ten-cup mold.
2. Line bottom with the chocolate ice cream. Sprinkle with black cherries.
3. Cover with 4 slices of sponge cake, and soak them with ¼ cup rum.
4. Top with vanilla ice cream and sprinkle with sliced banana.
5. Top again with sponge cake slices and soak with remaining ¼ cup rum.
6. Cover with wax paper and freeze at a very cold temperature for at least 6 hours.
7. Remove mold from freezer. Dip mold for 3 to 4 seconds in hot water. Discard wax paper, and run a knife around the sides of the mold. Reverse mold onto serving platter and knock sharply to release.

Serves 6 to 8

TORTA DI RISO   *Emilia-Romagna*
Brandy-Flavored Almond and Rice Torte

This very ancient cake (it was already fashionable at Renaissance banquets) is particularly traditional for the *feste degli addobbi*. The *addobbi*, from *addobbare* (to decorate) are the decennial feasts of the parish churches in Bologna. People repaint the facades of their houses and decorate them with damask draperies (the aristocratic families with their coat of arms on it), torches, garlands, and precious religious paintings for the procession. This cake is also traditional for the religious procession of the Madonna di San Luca. This is when the most venerated image of the Holy Virgin in Bologna (an icon—which legend wants to be painted by Saint Luke the Apostle—covered by a quantity of jewels and pearls) is carried down from her sanctuary on the Monte della Guardia, under miles of ancient colonnades, to the cathedral of San Pietro. In both cases (i.e., the *addobbi* and the procession of the Madonna) Brandy-Flavored Almond and Rice Torte is both sold on stands or served during parties and dinners given by the people whose houses border the route of the procession.

> *1 quart milk, hot*
> *¾ teaspoon salt*
> *1 cup uncooked long grain rice*
> *1 2½- by 1½-inch slice lemon peel plus ½ heaping teaspoon grated lemon peel*
> *2 2½- by 1½-inch slices orange peel plus ½ heaping teaspoon grated orange peel*
> *3 or 4 espresso coffee beans*
> *½ cup granulated sugar*
> *¼ teaspoon vanilla extract*
> *1½ cups crushed, blanched almonds*
> *2 eggs, lightly beaten*
> *2 egg yolks, lightly beaten*
> *½ cup good Cognac*
> *3 teaspoons Aurum or Grand Marnier*

1. Mix hot milk and salt in top of large double boiler, and place over moderately boiling water. Add the rice, sliced lemon and orange peels, and coffee beans. Cover loosely and steam, stirring very frequently with a fork, for approximately ½ hour, or until rice is tender and milk is absorbed. Remove from heat and let rice cool completely.

2. Preheat oven to 375° F.

3. When rice is cool, remove and discard lemon and orange peels and coffee beans. Add sugar, vanilla extract, almonds, beaten eggs, and egg yolks, ¼ cup of the Cognac, and the grated lemon and orange rinds. Mix thoroughly.

4. Pour mixture into well-buttered baking pan or pans to a height of no more than 1¼ inches. Bake in oven for 30 to 45 minutes, or until top is golden brown and a knife, inserted in the *torta,* comes out clean.

5. Remove from oven, prick top all over with a fork, and pour over it a mixture of the remaining Cognac and Aurum or Grand Marnier. Chill completely before cutting—traditionally in small lozenges.

SERVES 6 TO 8

CROCCANTE   *North Italy*
ALMOND BRITTLE

Croccante is the simplest sort of candy—the sort of thing Italian children make when they are first allowed in the kitchen—much as American children begin to experiment with fudge, although Croccante is simpler. But in addition to being a nutty goody children love, it is frequently crushed or pulverized and used as a lining or topping in more elaborate desserts.

1 teaspoon sweet butter
2 cups confectioners' sugar
2 tablespoons lemon juice
2 cups chopped, blanched almonds

1. Butter cookie sheet or platter.

2. In a saucepan mix sugar and lemon juice and stir, over low heat, until sugar is melted. Add the chopped almonds, and stir mixture until golden. Spread evenly, about ½ inch thick, with spatula, on buttered surface, cut into 2-inch-sized lozenges and let harden.

MAKES ABOUT 15 LOZENGES

AMARETTI   *Lombardy*
ALMOND MACAROONS

¼ teaspoon salt
2 egg whites
1 cup sugar
1 cup chopped, blanched almonds
¾ teaspoon almond extract
1 buttered and floured baking sheet

1. Add the salt to the egg whites, and beat until frothy.

2. Add sugar gradually, beating, until mixture is stiff but not dry. Add almonds and almond extract and fold in gently.

3. Drop almond mixture on buttered and floured baking sheet by the teaspoon, shape into ovals, leaving about 1 inch between each mound. Let stand about 2 hours.

4. Preheat oven to 375° F.

5. Bake macaroons for about 12 minutes, or until delicately brown in color.

MAKES ABOUT 25 MACAROONS

INDEX

INDEX